Born in 1959 in Hemel Hempstead, Dougie Brimson went directly into the RAF from school where he trained as a mechanical engineer. After serving for over eighteen years and attaining the rank of sergeant, he left the forces in 1994 to pursue a career as a writer. He is married to Tina and has three children.

Dougie Brimson and his brother Eddy are the co-authors of four books, *Everywhere We Go*, *England, My England*, *Capital Punishment* and *Derby Days* – all of which are published by Headline.

He has written a novel, *The Crew*, also published by Headline, and is currently working on his second novel, *Billy's Log*.

Barmy Army

The Changing Face
of Football Violence

Dougie Brimson

headline

First published in 2000
by HEADLINE BOOK PUBLISHING

10 9 8 7 6

ISBN 0 7472 6305 1

Typeset by Avon Dataset Ltd, Bidford-on-Avon, Warks

Printed and bound in Great Britain by
Mackays of Chatham plc, Chatham, Kent

HEADLINE BOOK PUBLISHING
A division of the Hodder Headline Group
338 Euston Road
London NW1 3BH

www.headline.co.uk
www.hodderheadline.com

306.483/BRI

Contents

————————

For Tina.

Acknowledgements

———————————————

With thanks to everyone who helped out with the research and who answered frantic phone calls or e-mails, especially Pat Nally, Dave (2), 'Joe Hawkins', Chris, Pete, Tim and all the lads from all the clubs who, together with everyone else, had best remain nameless! You all know who you are, though, and you were invaluable.

This book was written on a Pentium II computer supplied by CTX Computers Europe Ltd (01923 810800).

Introduction

A few years ago, I co-wrote a book. It wasn't the first of its type, not by any means, but thankfully it was, and continues to be, a reasonably good seller. Although I would like to believe that this success was entirely due to the fact that it is a bloody good book, it is fair to say that a good portion of it can be attributed to one very important factor: timing. The book, entitled *Everywhere We Go*, was about football hooliganism and was released in March 1996. Just over a year after rioting England fans had forced the abandonment of an international game in Dublin and a few short months before the start of the largest football tournament this country had staged for 30 years.

Such timing was no accident. And with a government terrified at the prospect of Euro 96 being remembered more for the violence surrounding it than the actual football, as well as a media seemingly intent on stirring up that violence, *Everywhere We Go* received a massive amount of attention when it was first published. Reviews ranged from 'probably the best book ever written on football violence' (*Daily Mail*) to simply 'fuck off' (*Time Out*) and to promote it we appeared on everything from breakfast television to local radio. As any publisher will tell you, such exposure is priceless and most authors would kill for the amount of publicity the book received.

One of the unique features of *Everywhere We Go* was the way it tackled the issue. Unlike the books written by some of the academic half-wits who study (sic) hooliganism, it contained no bullshit, exaggeration or patronising theory. It simply looked at every aspect of the problem and, where necessary, examined it using either experience, opinion or anecdotes. Nothing was held back, hidden or ignored; if it impacted on the problem, it was tackled, as directly and honestly as it could have been. The fact that we were prepared to appear in the media, and not only admit to being involved in the past but explain why, was a huge selling point and one which we exploited at every opportunity.

While the media response was one thing, the reaction from the public was simply amazing. For me, one of the aims had always been to write a book that, to use a well-worn phrase, told it how it was. Or to be more specific, how it had been for me. And as I was far from the stereotypical footie thug, or at least I believed I was, the hope was that by approaching it in that way, the book would expose many of the myths and stereotypes that surround hooliganism for the utter rubbish that they are. But the only way to be sure that the book achieved that aim was to invite direct comment from the people who read it. And so, on the back page, an address was included together with a plea for feedback.

Within weeks, letters were flooding in by the sackload. Some were supportive, some were astonished. A few were simply angry. But the one thing that came across most strongly to me was that my own experiences were so, well, typical. Indeed, the views and opinions expressed in the book, be they about hooliganism or any of the other issues examined such as policing or the right-wing influence, were similar to those of the vast majority of people who responded. If nothing else, that gave me a gratifying sense of achievement. It reaffirmed our assertion that we were simply two average football fans who had written a book.

But *Everywhere We Go* was not just about why hooliganism exists, it was about understanding the culture surrounding it, why people became involved and how, more importantly, we believed it could be stopped. As a result, much of the content centred around attacks on the press, the police and the football authorities for their role in the abject failure to deal with the hooligan menace which had, remember, already existed for over a century and had almost brought the game to its knees at one point. The fact that at that time the country was facing a bill of £10–20 million to police Euro 96 seemed to underline the point.

Naively, I believed that because our ideas for dealing with the problem were based on personal experience rather than academic study, someone in authority would want to hear them. After all, isn't the best person to ask about stopping car crime an ex-car thief? And if someone writes a book about an issue causing you major problems and that book sits high in the bestsellers list for a good few weeks, surely it might be worth having them in for a chat. But I was wrong. While the positive feedback from the public was most welcome, the people we really needed to respond remained silent. Not only that, but as Euro 96 approached and the tabloid press continued to clamour for quotes about organised gangs and possible riots, things began to happen that I was not prepared for.

Right from the outset, certain elements of the media had been critical of the book. That was fair enough; if you write anything for publication, you have to expect that and if you are controversial, it is fairly obvious that not everyone is going to agree with what you say or how you say it. However, most of the criticism was aimed not at the book itself but at the authors. Accusations that we were exploiting a violent past or making money on the back of that violence came pouring down – with, to be honest, some justification because we *were* making money. There were also allegations that we were glorifying violence or even, in a few cases, stirring it up. One magazine even hinted that *Everywhere We Go* had been ghost written and that we were simply a front for some-one else. At first, such things hurt, but I soon realised that many of the people who were critical of the book either hadn't even read it or were simply jealous because they hadn't thought of it first and resented its success. Furthermore, the old adage 'there is no such thing as bad publicity' quickly proved itself to be true. Each slagging led to more exposure and more sales, and if making money had been what it was really about then I'd have happily cultivated as much rumour as I could have. But making money wasn't what it was all about. And as the criticism continued, it soon became clear that any hopes we had that someone would listen to what we had to say were diminishing fast.

Ironically, while we were desperately trying to meet with the authorities, they began to take an unhealthy interest in what we were up to. Some phone calls were accompanied by so many clicks and buzzes that at times I almost started dancing. And through the simple ploy of sending spoof mail to ourselves, it quickly became clear that either the Royal Mail sorting offices were going through a particularly bad patch or someone was intercepting it. I also began to notice the same middle-aged faces popping up at various points on train journeys across London and despite the fact that they were always left secured, cars would be found unlocked when they were returned to. It was, to say the least, a total waste of someone's effort and resources.

Thankfully, with a few notable exceptions, the widespread public disorder it was feared would accompany Euro 96 never materialised and in the months that followed, a sequel to *Everywhere We Go* called *England, My England* was released to more media attention. However, as time passed, and a further two books were written, each looking at different aspects of the hooligan problem, one thing remained crystal clear. Despite huge amounts of effort and money on my part and more letters than I care to remember, any chance of kick-starting or even becoming involved with any kind of legitimate anti-hooligan campaign is zero. Over these last few years, the number of meetings I have had with anyone in any kind of authority amounts to two – and neither of them were in any way, shape or form, productive.

I can understand why that is, of course. As someone who admits to having been involved in hooliganism in the past, albeit on a very small scale, and who actually looks like the stereotypical football thug, I'm hardly the most attractive person to have sitting opposite you and there are no guarantees that anything I say would actually prove to be of any use. So why should they bother? When many people outside the game – and a few inside it – believe that hooliganism has apparently all but vanished from football, what purpose could be served by talking to someone who, on the face of it, has a vested interest on publicising the problem? It is a question I have been asked on numerous occasions and the answer is simple. It also explains why I am writing this book and what it's about.

To state the blindingly obvious, hooliganism evolves to keep ahead of authority. It has to, otherwise it would long since have ceased to be a problem. The more laws they bring in, the more intelligence the police get hold of, the more the hooligans will find ways round it all. It's what they do and, for many people, why they do it. But having talked at length about the build-up to Euro 96 recently, I was astonished at quite how much hooliganism has changed in these few short years. The growing use of technology to plan violence is one of the more obvious and worrying developments, but there was one thing that concerned me much more than that. It is possibly the most dangerous development of all and, somewhat ironically, one of the best indications of it can be found on the shelves of bookshops in every high street in the land.

Prior to the release of *Everywhere We Go*, there had actually been very few books about football violence. The majority of those that had been written were academic studies and the remainder exercises in nostalgia, propaganda or both, depending on your viewpoint. Colin Ward's *Steaming In* remains probably the best of the bunch, with Jay Allan's *Bloody Casuals* running it a close second. The other book from that period which comes readily to mind is *Among the Thugs* by Bill Buford, which I believe would be far more at home in the fiction department of the local bookshop than in the sport section where it can generally be found. However, all three books were hugely successful and, aside from the subject matter, they had one thing in common: they were written to entertain. No more, no less. And while that was certainly one of the objectives with *Everywhere We Go*, it was not the primary aim. If it had been, we would simply have filled a book with 101 great rucks and followed it up with 101 more great rucks. But we didn't, because we did not want to glorify for gratification, we wanted to expose and inform. So *Everywhere We Go* didn't just say 'we did this' or 'they did that', it said 'we did this because . . .' and, more importantly, 'but this might have stopped us'. It was this unique approach that brought a whole new dimension to the genre, and that isn't just my rose-tinted opinion either. To borrow a quote from *FourFourTwo* magazine when they reviewed the fourth book in the series, *Derby Days*, in 1998: '*Everywhere We Go* remains a watershed.'

However, once it hit the bookshops and became a success, one of the consequences I wasn't prepared for was the number of people who suddenly thought that writing about their own experiences would be a good idea. It is fair to say that as a direct result of the success of *Everywhere We Go*, the last few years have seen an explosion in the hooligan genre. Where once there were very few books about hooliganism, now there are shelves full of them. Football violence has become a marketable commodity and there is certainly a market for it. I'll take, and have taken, my share of flak about this. After all, there were three other books bearing my name after *Everywhere We Go*. But whereas they were all objective and critical in their approach, titles such as *England's Number One*, *Guv'nors* and *Hoolifan* are not. The motives for writing books such as those seem to me to be dubious and I would even go so far as to say that they worship thuggery. I find it not only ironic but offensive that I am frequently accused of glorifying football violence when books such as these are not only being written but are actually being promoted on the back of the writers' own brutality.

Aside from the glorification, my other big problem with

books such as these isn't that they are particularly bad, it's that they're pointless. They contribute nothing to the debate and you will find very few, if any, examinations, explanations or apologies in any of them. Just fight after fight after fight, very few of which, funnily enough, involve the writers actually getting hurt. What's more, they paint a particular and dangerous version of the past, one in which kicking the shit out of someone lying on the floor was fun. But of course, it wasn't, not if you were the one on the floor. It was the worst kind of crap. One also wonders how much the stories in some of these books have 'improved' in the telling, if they actually took place at all.

To be fair, the accusation of glorification could be levelled at my last book, *The Crew*, because that does glorify certain aspects of hooliganism, as do John King's excellent novel *The Football Factory* and Kevin Sampson's *Awaydays*. But the essential difference here is that *The Crew*, *Awaydays* and *The Football Factory* are fiction; *Everywhere We Go* and the others I wrote with Eddy were all fact. And while fiction is one thing and non-fiction another, fiction masquerading as non-fiction is something else entirely. Indeed, *The Football Factory* can actually be found residing in the sport section of some bookshops rather than the fiction department, which says as much for the marketing department of its publisher as it does about the content of the book.

The fact that these autobiographical accounts are being written and published is a sign that attitudes to football violence are changing. People are reading these nostalgic, rose-tinted versions of history and referring to the terrace battles and smashed-up trains of the 70s and 80s as 'the good old days'. And the more they do that, the more acceptable the culture of hooliganism becomes, and so it grows. Even NCIS, the National Criminal Intelligence Service, admits that. And as it grows, the more enticing it becomes. The attraction of belonging to a gang draws in new followers to the cause, with the result that the mobs get bigger and you need more police to police them. The more police you have, the more interesting the game of hooliganism becomes. And so it goes on, it's self-perpetuating.

That this is happening scares the shit out of me, and so that is what this book is about; the changing face of hooliganism. It will examine how and why those changes have come about and will take a fresh look at the causes of hooliganism, which, like the methods, have changed significantly in recent years. More importantly, it will examine what can be done to change the attitudes both of those who fight and those who deny even that such people still exist (because to my mind each is as big a problem as the other). This book will also ask searching questions of both the government and the football authorities as well as level accusations of both negligence and incompetence.

Once again, I have written it in the hope that it will get people thinking about aspects of the hooligan issue that they may not necessarily have considered before. If it achieves that, then maybe the game will wake up to the reality of football hooliganism and do something about it, because at the moment, no one seems to realise that these changes are happening and nothing is being done to combat it. Forget all the crap about police intelligence and new legislation; that's all meaningless, party-political hype. The truth is that no one in authority is addressing the root causes of hooliganism because they have no direct experience of it and simply do not understand it. How can they, when even I, after many seasons on the terraces, six books and years of research, am genuinely shocked and astonished at some of the things I get told?

I should however make two things clear straight away. First, this book is not *Everywhere We Go 2*. It is called *Barmy Army* for a specific reason, and one which I will talk about later. Second, some of what is contained in this book may seem familiar not just from the books I have been involved with but from others. The reason for that is simply that to explain the background to this issue, you have to understand the history. And history is constant, even though individual slants on it may vary.

What I will stress, however, is that everything contained within these pages has been checked and double-checked to the best of my ability and resources. I know full well that many people will regard what I write here as at best insincere and at worst pure bullshit. But all I can say is that nothing is made up or fabricated by me and if an anecdote is included, it is genuine and I have the original letter, e-mail or tape right here in my office.

One thing that may surprise some people is that some of my own opinions and views have changed, or at least modified. For example, initially, while I condemned the hooligan groups and everything they did, my approach was very much a case of 'they're doing it, so stop them'. To a degree, this missed one vital point and it was one that on occasions was maybe not made forcibly enough: the hooligans are responsible for all this. If they did not continue to cause problems at games, there would be no need for segregation, early kick-offs or CCTV. Clubs would not be forced to pay out huge amounts of income on policing their games and when England play abroad, television news crews would not be salivating at the prospect of serious violence on foreign streets. We should not forget that the blame for all of that, and more, lies squarely on those Stone Island and Burberry-clad shoulders.

However, there is one opinion that has not changed. Ultimately, the responsibility for dealing with the hooligans lies not with the forces of law and order but with the game they follow. The FA and the clubs have a duty, as well as the power, to bring about a resolution to the hooligan problem, but it is a duty they have largely ignored and a power they have refused to wield. Instead, for years the game has tried to sweep this issue under the carpet and it simply cannot carry on doing that for much longer. Sooner or later, unless something is done, we're going to have a repeat of Dublin or worse in this country. I feel guilty enough about my part in the problem already. I don't want that on my conscience as well.

Because it is my fault. Or more accurately, it is the fault of me and people like me because as I have already mentioned, I used to be involved in trouble at games. Not much, but a little. And so, in effect, I was a part of the very problem I am talking about. And before we get into the nitty gritty of this book, it is important that I go over my own involvement so that there is no doubt about my own 'credentials'. Primarily because they, together with my motives, have been called into question on more than one occasion.

Funnily enough, I never regarded myself as a hooligan. Just a fan or, at worst, a bit of a lad. Indeed, as a resumé of football violence, what follows is pretty tame compared to many and I most certainly never was a 'top boy' at any club, nor have I ever claimed to be. But while I am glad that my own involvement was limited, I must also stress that I am not ashamed of any of the things I did.

I'm not proud of them either, mind, but I cannot deny that I enjoyed running with a little mob. It is an incredibly exciting thing to be involved in. That may seem something of a paradox, given that I am writing a book about how football violence is a problem, but it is how I feel. What I became involved in was wrong, I readily admit that, and if I had my time again I might well do things differently. But you can't change the past, all you can do is learn from it, and try to stop others from repeating your mistakes.

My earliest recollection of football as a professional sport probably dates back to 1964. My dad, being a post-war refugee from Tottenham, was a Spurs fan and I can vividly remember standing in the garden of my grandparents' house in Waltheof Avenue, N17, listening to the noise of the crowd coming from White Hart Lane one Saturday afternoon. Despite my pleas, however, he never took me to see them play, an omission that was to have a major influence on my supporting life.

I started going to football when I was about nine. The first game I actually saw in the flesh was in the 1968–69 season between Watford and Bristol Rovers at Vicarage Road. It was, I recall, a 1–0 win for the Hornets but it was freezing cold and the game was total crap. As a result, I avoided football for a while and settled into life as a speedway and stock car fan, travelling each week with various neighbours to tracks around the south east. However, after the 1970 FA Cup final, I, like many lads of that era, fell in love with Chelsea. Peter Osgood's diving header showed me how exciting football could be and by the time Dave Webb headed in the winning goal, I knew that I had to see them play. As a result, I became what I suppose we would now call a scarfer. And although I began paying the odd visit to Vicarage Road, my heart at that time was with Ossie at the Bridge. By the end of 1973, I stopped fighting it and became almost a regular on the left-hand side of the Shed, standing there with a fellow Chelsea fan from my school in the days when Chelsea wore a second strip of green, red and white. At least once a month, we would travel to West London and watch as chaos reigned. It was awesome; and that was just inside. Outside was mayhem! We even did a couple of away trips, the first to Charlton and the second to QPR. It seemed that every time we went, something would happen to scare the shit out of us but as soon as we could, we would go back. The problem was, the more we went, the braver we got and one day we ended up standing almost, but not quite, in the middle of the Shed.

To this day, I don't know who Chelsea were playing, nor if the opposition's fans had managed to infiltrate the hallowed terrace, but what I do know is that I was standing on the Shed minding my own business when a full-bore riot kicked off right in front of me. Men fought with chains, clubs, the lot and eventually the police sent the dogs in. Even that didn't stop them and in the end some of them began waving knives around within inches of us. For my mate, that was it. It was too scary and although I went back on my own once, and was chased around Euston by some Arsenal fans for my trouble, I stopped going to the Bridge after that. The only kind of boy I ever got to be at Chelsea was a 15-year-old one.

Vicarage Road, and especially the Rookery, became my footballing home after that and although I was hardly a regular, I was a frequent visitor. Trouble was something we rarely saw at the Vic in those days, primarily because Watford were languishing in the lower depths of the league, but thanks largely to the *News of the World* I was able to keep my eye on events in West London. After I left home and joined the RAF in 1975, I resigned myself to the fact that trips to Watford home games would be almost impossible. But thankfully, a year later I was posted to a camp in Aylesbury and returned to the fray. By now violence at games was becoming commonplace, even at Watford. Each week the papers would be full of all kinds of mayhem and it seemed that every club who came to Vicarage Road tried something on. As a member of Her Majesty's Armed Forces I felt duty bound to maintain a discreet distance, mostly due to the fear that I would be thrown out of the RAF if I was ever arrested. I was still an avid crowd-watcher but if I did find myself in trouble, I was out of there. One such incident involved West Ham in 1979, when they paid their first ever league visit to our ground. To let us know who was boss, they infiltrated every section of Vicarage Road and 'announced their presence' in the traditional way as the teams ran out. I was sat in the middle of about 50 of their lads with a mate who had the thickest Bristol accent you have ever heard and two girls, one of whom was from Yorkshire and both of whom were attending their first ever game. As a pulling tool it was not a success.

Very occasionally, however, trouble was unavoidable. My training in the forces had equipped me with certain useful skills, some of which were various methods of rendering people helpless and getting away from them. The first time I was called upon to employ this expertise was in the away end at Loftus Road at a game which didn't even involve Watford at all. For reasons that are buried in my memory, I hadn't travelled to watch the Hornets and so I joined a carload of fellow servicemen and headed for Upton Park. Unfortunately, the car broke down and by the time we had fixed it, the only game we could make before kick-off time was QPR–Liverpool. As one of our number was a Scouser and I have an aversion to Rangers – a legacy of my away trip with Chelsea – we decided to go in the Liverpool end, a decision we were to regret almost instantly. One of the lads we had with us was black, and although no one said anything, it was clear that his presence had been noted and was unwelcome. At half-time we went to the toilet and as we came out, he was suddenly surrounded by a group of Scouse kids who all demanded money off him. His response was immediate and to the negative but they persisted and began shoving the two of us. I may be a fat git now, but back then I was fit as a fiddle and the lad with me was heavily into weight training and built like a brick shithouse. In fact, his physique made parts of Loftus Road look positively rickety. A few swift clouts and the young Scouse gits vanished only to be replaced immediately by decidedly older Scouse gits. Amazingly, we managed to fight our way out and dived over the barriers and onto the pitch before being escorted round to the home end. But it was desperate and decidedly scary stuff.

The next occasion was only a few weeks later when I became involved in a bizarre incident with some Fulham fans in a graveyard in the centre of Watford. I was on my way back to the station after the game, taking a short cut across the tomb stones, when this little mob steamed in and began hitting out at anyone they could reach. I was on the far side of the yard and began moving away but when I saw one of them hit an old man and knock him to the floor, I saw red and steamed across. By the time the Old Bill arrived, I had this guy on the deck with his arm up his back but the police grabbed me and tried to haul me away, leaving him to stand up and walk off. Thankfully, the old boy who had been attacked managed to get their attention and with a flash of the ID card, a tool that was to become increasingly useful as time passed, I was released and sent on my way.

In the early 80s, as my career and a posting to Germany took over, my involvement with English football petered out for a while, although when I was home on leave I attended as many games as I could and travelled around with the same lads. However, when, after two years abroad, I was posted back to England at the start of 1982, a number of things happened that were to have a major effect on my supporting life.

The first of these was that when I came back from Germany, it was to a unit in Oxfordshire. As luck would have it, the camp already had a resident contingent of Hornets and so I immediately became a part of the match-day exodus to Vicarage Road. The second thing was that in April that year, Argentina invaded the Falklands and as an expert in aircraft crash recovery with recent Harrier experience, I was immediately put on 24-hour stand-by to go. The third and most important thing was that I caught the arse end of one of the great seasons in Watford's history. Graham Taylor had got the team working as a fantastic unit and, although none of us knew it, we were on the verge of great things. Promotion was secured at home to Wrexham and after a final home fixture against Leicester City, we travelled to Derby County for the final game secure in the knowledge that we would finish as runners-up and, for the first time in our history, would start the next season in the First Division.

But we didn't leave the Second without saying good-bye. Our season may have been over but Derby's most certainly was not. They needed to win to stay up and it was clear that the mood at the Baseball Ground would be hostile. For the first time, or at least the first time I had seen, Watford took a serious mob to an away game and went on the offensive. But while the Hornets hordes were certainly ready for trouble, our mood was not helped by the police, who gave what I can only describe as a shameful example of their profession. On the walk from the train station to the ground, they were simply rude and abusive. Once they got us inside, supporters were verbally and physically abused, fingers poked through fences were hit with truncheons and as officers walked along the perimeter they repeatedly kicked stones into the faces of the people in the packed visitors' enclosure. By the time half-time arrived, the Watford contingent were almost rabid. Fences were pulled down and missiles were hurled. Then outside, after the game, the fans just went ballistic. The worst incident of many involved a mounted policeman who fell off his horse when it reared up as the Watford mob tried to get past it. He caught one of his feet in the stirrups and as the animal tried to get away, the policeman was dragged along while the crowd kicked seven bells out of him. The Watford fans caused mayhem that day and as an interested observer, I was astonished that supporters of my club could do so much damage to both people and property.

Three days later, I was on a plane heading south as part of Maggie's Task Force. Thankfully, the Argies rolled over pretty quickly and I was back just in time to catch the start of what was to be a historic season. I put the events of the South Atlantic, not to mention the Baseball Ground, to one side and swore that I would attend every game, home and away. A difficult undertaking at the best of times, as most football fans will appreciate, but when you throw in the various duties servicemen have to undertake, some of which last two weeks at a stretch, it was a daunting task. However, thanks to the support of a decent boss, and lots of wheeling and dealing on the duties front, I was certain that I could do it and by the time the fixture list was published, I was raring to go. And who wouldn't have been, faced with trips to some of the biggest clubs in the land?

But as the season approached, we began to hear rumblings from the supporters of other clubs, most of which were far from friendly. My home town was full of Chelsea, Spurs, West Ham and Arsenal fans and among them were some especially nasty mobs. Whereas before they had always looked upon Watford as a quaint little local side, now we were in direct opposition to their own clubs and many of them made it quite clear that as far as they were concerned, we were going to spend the season getting put firmly in our place.

The season started astonishingly. The team rampaged through the division and soon settled in the top half of the table. But apart from the odd scuffle on away trips, we had no real trouble – something that was to change dramatically when we went to Bolton for a League Cup tie in October. On a night of torrential rain, the local lads flashed more knives around than I had ever seen, and we shat it. The coppers were as bad as their lads. When we protested, their response was simply, 'Well, you shouldn't have come up here then should you, you Cockney cunts.' We learnt a lot that night, the most important lesson being that Bolton were bloody animals!

A couple of weeks later, the Watford fans faced their first big test. It was a game we had been looking forward to for decades, Spurs at White Hart Lane. We had already been told that Spurs would turn us over, but on the day we took thousands down and all we saw of their mob was a few of them shadowing us as we were escorted to the ground. Apart from that, nothing. It was an anticlimax, but three weeks later we travelled to Highbury and got our first serious taste of First Division trouble. This was one of the games I had been most concerned about, because one of the worst mobs in my home town had sworn that they would have a go at us. I wasn't alone in that feeling and, as a result, we bottled it a bit and decided that rather than go on the train, we would all travel down by coach. We arrived on the Clock End just after two o'clock to find that the place was already rammed, but by about 2.45 it became apparent that a large mob of Arsenal had arrived in the end and were firmly ensconced at the back. Worrying though this was, it was clear that the Watford lads were more than up for it.

I was stood about halfway down the terrace, leaning on a crush barrier with a pie in one hand and a cup of coffee in the other, when it kicked off. I can't say who started it but Watford were soon on top. Attacking up the terrace, their sheer weight of numbers coupled with some ferocious fighting drove the Arsenal fans along the top towards the exits. Suddenly, a hand came out of nowhere and grabbed hold of my arm. I turned to find a middle-aged woman screaming at me to get up the back and help my mates. I looked at her for a second, totally shocked, and then handed her my cup, stuffed what was left of the pie in my mouth, ducked under the barrier and headed for the back. But as soon as I stood up, a police-man appeared right in front of me and hit me full on the chin. In between the stars I was seeing, I heard him shout, 'Stay there, you cunt, I'll be back for you in a minute!' and he vanished. But I couldn't move, even if I wanted to. I simply fell back against the barrier and tried to remember where I was. By the time I had regained some sense of feeling in my head, the ruck was over and the Arsenal lads had been banished. It was a massive result and although we expected them to have a go outside, they were nowhere to be seen after the game and we didn't see any more trouble at all.

As the weeks passed, and the team were exceeding all expectations, we travelled the country and made a nuisance of ourselves all over. At Anfield, for example, some Scousers came into our end thinking they could take the piss and were battered senseless. However, things didn't always go our way and we were occasionally on the receiving end of a few slaps. Nothing major, but enough to warrant a few white lies to explain various bruises when I went into work on a Monday morning. But as Christmas 1982 approached, fate threw another curve at me, this time in the shape of a woman. Without going into it all too deeply, I knew immediately that one day we would be married. It would only be a matter of weeks before she had a major effect on my activities.

As the season moved into 1983, our little mob of about 20 lads had yet to come up against any serious opposition and we began to think we were better than we were. We started to take risks, and in February we took one that was to have major, and painful, consequences, especially for me. The incident concerned has already been written about in *Everywhere We Go*, so I will not go over it again in much depth. Suffice to say that rather than go by train or coach with the other lads, I took my car and three others down to Watford's game at Swansea and had the living shit kicked out of me. So much so that when I eventually made it into work on the Monday morning, I had to tell everyone I had been a passenger in a car that had been involved in an accident. Two days later, I found out I had three broken ribs. Despite that, the next weekend we took a mob down to Spurs, where Swansea were playing, to try and exact revenge. But they didn't show and we just ended up leaving early to avoid any trouble from the locals. More seriously, the Monday after the trip to Spurs, my fledgling girlfriend found blood on the passenger seat and, putting two and two together, came up with a perfect four. She was not best pleased and although she never tried to stop me going to football, I knew that she was worried every time I headed for a game. I now began to think seriously about what I was risking every time I went to football and pushed my luck. But with the club doing so well, I just couldn't stop going and in March we travelled to Coventry for what most people who were there regard as one of our finest hours.

After the Swansea match, I had learnt my lesson and so travelled on a coach with the other lads. For some reason, the police put us in the side of the ground, well away from the rest of the Watford contingent and in an unsegregated section that included a good number of local lads, none of whom were pleased to see us. As the game progressed, the locals began to creep over to us and in the end, we were surrounded by a mob that not only looked decidedly nasty but also outnumbered us by about two to one. This quickly led to a couple of minor offs but we stood our ground and the police simply pushed us apart and stood watching while tensions mounted. When Watford scored what proved to be the winner, we went mental, which did their mood no good at all, but aside from a few more verbals, not much else happened. Once the game finished, the police took the locals away and kept us in the ground for about 15 minutes, but instead of hanging around we escaped around the back of the goal and down a steep set of stairs into the street. The second the last one of us was through the gates, the stewards slammed them shut behind us and we suddenly realised we were in the shit. There wasn't a copper in sight and blocking our way were the lot we had been winding up and a good number of their mates. To say the odds were stacked against us is an understatement, and when they began to move towards us we could see that unless we acted, we were in for a major hammering. So we did the only thing we could, we went for it. The shout went up and as one we steamed across the road towards them. I don't know what they must have thought but as we got near them, most of them bottled it and did the off while the rest were thrown over gardens or simply slapped to the ground. We chased them for a while and then turned round to go back to the coach park, but by then the ones we had gone through had regrouped and were now blocking our way. With everyone on a major high, we needed no second invitation. We steamed back in and ran them for a second time and by the time we got back to the coach park, we were buzzing. When a few of them appeared on the other side of a fence and began throwing rocks from a railway line, we simply unleashed a volley of missiles at them and they vanished.

The journey home was something else. Although some of the lads had picked up a few bruises, most of us were unscathed and the atmosphere on the coach was amazing. It had been, as far as we were concerned, a major result. After all, we had been away from home and outnumbered, but had run their firm twice in a matter of minutes. For us, it didn't get any better than that.

For the next few weeks, we became an even bigger pain in the arse than we had been and played up whenever the opportunity arose. But with the team doing so well, it was hard not to get caught up in the euphoria surrounding that and I became increasingly wrapped up in what was happening on the pitch as opposed to off it.

Around the same time, other things began to influence

my behaviour on match days. In particular, the RAF handed me the opportunity to convert to permanent flying duties. For most blokes, this is a dream job and I was no exception. But I could not run the risk of anything approaching damage to my service record and so I began to step back from trouble altogether. I had never been the first one in but now I was usually among the last, that's if I made it at all. Word of our activities was spreading through the hooligan grapevine and clubs were making stronger efforts to turn us over, so by the time Easter weekend approached, with two of the biggest games of the season in the space of 48 hours, I had already made the decision that once the season was over, I would give up away travel and simply go to home games as a fan.

On the Saturday, against all my instincts, I took my girlfriend with me to Upton Park and stood on the home end. Watching the Watford lads getting grief at the other end was not an enjoyable experience and nor was listening to some of the abuse Luther Blissett and John Barnes received from the locals. The fact that I arrived home in one piece was small comfort and I vowed I would never do such a cowardly thing again. Thankfully, just two days later, I had a chance to redeem myself.

Up to that point, violence at games had always involved at best apprehension, at worst outright terror. That was to change when, for the first and only time, I experienced what I could only describe at the time as blood lust, but which I later referred to as 'The Buzz'. Inevitably, it involved a club that I had already grown to detest, Watford's local and very bitter rivals L*t*n T*wn.

Watford's home end had long since moved out of the Rookery and was now at the other end of the ground, the Red Lion end, a huge, sprawling uncovered terrace. Some L*t*n fans had already been caught inside and slapped around a bit and the police had announced that they would be kept in after the game. Although by this time many clubs around the country had named mobs, at Watford no such thing existed. There were various small groups from places as diverse as Garston, Chorley and Hemel Hempstead, but although we all knew each other, it was rare that we actually stood together at home. Indeed, some of the groups didn't even get on. However, once the actual game had finished, word went round the entire end that we were going for it and everyone was to hang back. Within about five minutes, there were about 150 lads there, all wound up and ready. Suddenly a shout went up and before I knew it, I was in the middle of this pack steaming towards the junction of Vicarage Road and Merton Road, where L*t*n would emerge after being led round the allotments behind their end. As soon as we saw them, that was it, all hell broke loose. Initially, they ran and ended up in St Mary's Road, where they stopped and fronted us up. After the initial pause we surged forward and, grabbing anything we could out of the front gardens on either side, unleashed a hail of missiles at them. They responded and, after a few minutes, we surged forward and the fighting started. Eventually, the police arrived in force and drove us apart, forcing the L*t*n fans down the road and off towards the town centre and the train station. But we weren't finished yet. We pulled back and ran the short distance along Merton Road to Market Street, which runs parallel to St Mary's Road, our plan being to hit them again in the centre of town. But as we got halfway down, the police appeared in front of us and formed a line right across the road. Clearly, there was no way through and so we turned to go back, only to find that the police had got in behind us as well. We were now effectively sealed in Market Street with nowhere to go. They kept us there for what seemed an age, releasing us only when the L*t*n were on trains out of town and the effects of adrenaline had worn off.

As we walked slowly back to my car, I realised then exactly what I was risking and decided enough was enough. Although I continued to go to every game until the end of that season, and carried on for a good deal of the next, my days as a so-called hooligan were all but over. There were still the odd times when it was unavoidable, but they were rare and if I could, I would talk my way out of trouble rather than scrap. The only real exception to that came in 1987. By this time, I had married my girlfriend and was back in Germany and although still keeping an eye on Watford, had not been to a game for almost a year. Then it was announced that England would come to Dusseldorf for a friendly. Not only that, but I was given a free ticket. With the European Championships on the horizon, and English clubs still banned from Europe following the deaths of almost 40 Juventus fans caused by rioting Scousers at Heysel, every serviceman was given a severe warning about what would happen if they were involved in trouble at the game. However, largely thanks to the actions of the English media, a subject we will look at in depth later on, trouble kicked off outside the stadium after the game and I am ashamed to say I was caught up in it. Thankfully, I managed to get away without being detained, but I have not been involved in any trouble at games since.

Instead, like many people who were once involved, I became an interested observer. I began to keep track of who was up to what, but I also began to think about the hows and whys. Being in the forces helped, of course. I had lads from all over the country working for me and most of the ones who were into football had either been involved themselves at some point or knew people who had. And when you get sent somewhere like the Falklands for four months, there isn't much else to do except drink and reminisce.

By the time I left the forces in 1994, trouble at games was widely believed to be a thing of the past. Hillsborough had been the apparent catalyst for change and now we had a whole new type of football – all-seater stadia and corporate money. Motorway service stations positively welcomed football fans instead of barring them and the high streets of England were safe on Saturday afternoons. The hooligan was, as far as most people were concerned, history.

This was, as any football fan of the time will tell you, bullshit. I still went to games when I could and all too often ran a gauntlet of hate. But where once I enjoyed the atmosphere that accompanies confrontation and the apprehension that goes with away travel, now I was just sick of it. I saw the police becoming not far short of an army without weapons and I began to believe that football could be better than this. And so it could be, if the police weren't needed, if we didn't have to be segregated, and if we could walk into a pub on match day and be welcomed by the opposing fans instead of risking a kicking, or worse, for no other reason than that we support different teams.

I realised that back in 1994, but no one seemed to be doing anything about it. And so, on a sunny afternoon in Bristol, the idea for *Everywhere We Go* was born. To try to write a book that explained not only what we believed being a hooligan was all about but what could be done to stop people from becoming involved in it. The rest, as they say, is history.

PART ONE
The Demon In Our Midst

Chapter 1
Why?

———————————————

That is, of course, the wrong question. People should not ask *why* people indulge in hooliganism at games, they should ask why *can* they? When well over a century has passed since an incident of football violence at a game in England was first recorded and over 30 years has elapsed since it exploded onto the front pages of the popular press, why has so little been done to stop it? That is the big question, and one we will return to later on.

However, the question of why people go to football and cause trouble is one I have been asked more than any other over the last four years. While it is not impossible to answer, it is bloody difficult, primarily because most of the people who ask it believe it is nothing more complicated than a few lads running around getting mouthy or slapping each other. It is, of course, far more complex than that but if you are to supply an answer, it is important to understand that whatever you eventually come up with has to be a generalisation. I mean, if you get 20,000 people in a ground, you're always going to get two of them who don't agree, but what makes an individual suddenly decide that jumping onto the pitch and attacking a linesman is a good idea? And why do people get off on travelling to places under the banner of their club and actually go looking for trouble? How can you understand, let alone explain, that kind of mentality?

Before we get into that, we really have to ask another more specific question: what actually constitutes football hooliganism? Or to put it another way, what is a football hooligan?

To some, a hooligan will be something as simple and innocent as a teenage kid in a replica shirt walking along singing. But to others, it will be a lad who starts off a hit by hurling a CS gas canister through a plate glass window. An individual's perception of what constitutes a hooligan can only be decided in one of two ways: either by his or her own experiences or through the media. And it is fair to say that for many people who have no interest in football, let alone any experience of football violence, the stereotypical shaven-headed, racist thug so beloved of the tabloid press has become so ingrained in their perception of football fans that the two are almost inseparable. That is tragic, not only for the game but for every decent, law-abiding football fan in this country.

But for those who have actually tasted the rough end of football hooliganism, whether they are fans of the game themselves or not, their perception will be all too real. Anyone who has ever been confronted with a baying mob knows how frightening it can be, but if you are unprepared for it, it must be absolutely terrifying. Only recently, I met a man who told me of an incident he had found himself caught up in a few years ago. He asked to remain anonymous for obvious reasons, but even as we spoke it was clear that this had had a profound effect on him. What made it worse was that he has no interest in football at all.

I had been at a meeting in London all day and having been taken out to dinner by the client, had drunk too much wine to drive home so took the train. It was late, about 10.30, and I was sitting alone in a carriage at Euston waiting for the train to pull out when this group of men got on. There were about 15 of them, I suppose, all about 20–21, and although they were smartly dressed, even I could tell that they were football fans. A few other people got on as well and one of them was this lad of about 14 wearing a football shirt. Anyway, once the train pulled out, they started singing songs – nothing really abusive, just a bit colourful. But after a minute or so, a couple of them moved over towards this lad and started giving him a bit of grief. He supported a rival club, I suppose. He stood up to move away from them, but one of them shoved him back down and started being even more abusive. Eventually, one of them hit him and he started crying and so this other man got up to tell them to leave him alone. Well that was it, they started on him and he was punched in the face for his trouble, while all these other lads were just laughing. They then became even more abusive and some of the things they were saying to the women were outrageous. Yet despite the fact that I watched all this, I did nothing to stop it and, when they got off, I felt not just embarrassed but totally humiliated. The looks the women on the train gave me were of outright disgust and I couldn't get off there fast enough.

Now I hate bullying, and that's what this was.

> And even after all this time, I am ashamed that I didn't do anything to stop what was happening and it made me take a long, hard look at myself, that's for sure. I know I could never sit by and watch something like that again. But if that's what football is about for these people, then they can keep it. I can't even watch the game now without thinking of that night.

This incident illustrates perfectly the consequences of hooliganism in terms of public perception. The lads involved would probably have forgotten all about it by the time they were off the platform, yet for the people on the train that must have been a terrifying experience, and one which will have tainted their view of football fans forever.

But it is fairly accurate to say that incidents such as this involving active football hooligans are becoming rarer. One of the reasons for that is that hooliganism has developed into a 'game' with specific rules and a certain code of honour. The people involved tend to shy away from such encounters with the general public and are interested only in confronting each other, because there is nothing to be gained in terms of status or reputation from being aggressive towards innocent members of the public or even other, non-violent football fans.

It wasn't always thus. In the 60s, 70s and even the early 80s, one of the main objectives of the travelling mobs was to terrify the locals. Steaming down high streets and smashing windows was the norm for many groups of fans on match days and I well remember banner headlines in the *News of the World* sometime in the early 70s registering outrage at the fact that a gang of Chelsea fans had taken a pram containing a baby from outside a shop and steamed off up the road with it. These days, the focus has shifted from the local population as a whole to the opposing mobs and hooliganism has become a far more insular and underground beast. Consequently, the individual lads' perception of their own role in it has changed. For example, as I have already mentioned, I may have been involved in trouble at games but I never regarded myself as a hooligan. To me, hooligans were the boys who travelled around looking for it, hunting around back streets for opposing fans or hurling missiles at us from pub doorways. But to the locals, watching me from behind net curtains as I ran around, that was exactly what I was.

The simple answer to this question of defining football hooliganism is that it is a blanket term that can be applied to any kind of anti-social behaviour which damages the image of football, be it foul and abusive chanting or 50 lads ambushing a pub using baseball bats. As a descriptive word it is valuable only to the media and ranting MPs, but as a culture it is of interest to us all. Because if you ever end up in court for a football-related offence, be it drunk and disorderly or affray, the fact that the culture exists, and you are a part of it, will have major repercussions for you in terms of the sentence you receive. For many people, of course, the allure of the hooligan culture is what drew them into it in the first place. In the 'caring, sharing' 90s, it is almost unique in that it lets the average male behave in a manner that is totally at odds with what is normally expected of them.

We will look at why and how individuals become involved in hooliganism in the next chapter, but first we should look at what it is about football that invokes such emotions in people that they will willingly indulge in intimidation, violence and even murder in its name. Just as importantly, why football and not any other sport? After all, if what we are led to believe is correct, hooliganism is unique to football, and other sports are watched in an atmosphere of tranquil serenity devoid of any aggression at all. The truth is that almost every other mainstream sport has crowd problems of sorts. Admittedly, such problems are usually minor and in most cases of an entirely different nature to football, but they are problems nevertheless. Cricket has had some major problems with crowd trouble in recent years, primarily at internationals but also at county level, as has boxing. The fact that it happens but is rarely reported is simply because, in general, it is not newsworthy. Football has a long, dark history of crowd trouble and also, let's be honest, more of it. But we should not hide the fact that it takes place elsewhere, although the governing bodies of many of these sports are quite happy that we do so.

So what is it about football that makes it the focus of all this? Why can 22 men running around chasing a ball cause so many problems? To explain that, we need to examine what being a supporter is all about because, in part, that will supply the answer.

Football is the most popular sport on the planet. As kids we play it, at home we are forcefed it via TV, newspapers or obsessed parents, and eventually a good number of us go to watch it. As fans, our links with our chosen club, be it Bath City or Manchester City, rapidly become a part of our personality to such an extent that many football fans, me included, regard themselves as an integral and essential element of their club and the club as an essential part of them. We use expressions such as 'I'm a Gooner' in the same manner as we say 'I'm an engineer' and expect people to know just what that means (which, of course, they usually do!). Our clubs are followed through thick and thin and we accept the bad times in the hope that one day, the good ones will come along. In short, we support their efforts on our behalf. Yes, we hand over our money at the turnstiles but we also bring with us something that money cannot buy: passion.

The passion generated by supporters is what breathes life into a football club. Many supporters believe, with some justification, that they are its heart and soul. The players and the staff are simply passing through and will be gone one day, but they, as fans, will carry the aspirations of their club with them until their dying day. That may sound dramatic if you're not a football fan, but it is uncannily accurate. We want our clubs to be the best of the best and the dream is that one day they will be. More importantly, when it happens, we want to claim our part of it and say we did our bit. That's why football fans resent those who jump on bandwagons. Anyone can suddenly come out and say they support Arsenal or Manchester United, but they are not true supporters. They are simply hijacking the loyalty shown by others and riding along on the back of current success. Don't get me wrong, I've often whiled away a boring 0–0 draw against clubs like Bury or Rotherham wondering why I support Watford and not Arsenal. But I know that you can't just change clubs because times are bad. Do that and you have no right to enjoy the good times or, for that matter, to call yourself a true fan. Being a football supporter isn't about watching great football, it's about putting time in and belonging to something, the entity that is a football club. And that club isn't just a grass field and 11 men, it's much, much more than that. It's about history and tradition. That's why people go to watch clubs like Barnet and

Torquay United, and that's why football fans throughout the country unite when a club is about to go under. We may not understand why they support a different club from us, but they are our soulmates and we need to protect each other, because no one else will.

But inevitably, where you have passion and pride, you have rivalry. If you want your club to be the best, then at some point they will have to defeat others. Football is, after all, a competitive sport. And so supporters will sing, chant and shout to spur their team on in the hope that they will react and do the business on their behalf. Not only that, but on occasions the actions of the supporters can have a major influence on events on the pitch. The fans can, literally, earn the club a result, as Mick from Birmingham explains:

We were playing Tranmere at St Andrews a couple of season ago and as anyone knows, they have always been a dirty bunch of cunts. Anyway, one of their players took a dive right in front of the Kop and got one of our lads booked. What was worse was that when he got up, he had this fucking great grin on his face. Well, we all saw that and we went mental at this twat from then on. Every time he touched the ball we gave him shit and in the end, he bottled it. His crosses were going all over the fucking place and he had a bloody nightmare. In the end, he was subbed and I tell you what, as that cunt walked off, we gave ourselves the biggest fucking cheer of the day. The team won in the end and Trevor Francis went in the paper and said the crowd had made a massive difference. It made us feel fucking great, I can tell you.

_____

At the other end of the ground are a group of rival fans, who also aspire to victory. They will also be singing and shouting, and so you get atmosphere. Generally that atmosphere is good-natured but on occasions, as we have just seen, it can spill over into hostility or worse. Something happens on the pitch, a bad foul or a crap decision, and the mood will go from jovial to aggressive. Usually that aggression will quickly evaporate as soon as the final whistle goes, or if it doesn't, it will only show in bad moods or moaning. As you walk away from the ground, the smiles will return and by the time you're in the pub or the car, it will almost be forgotten. After all, you cannot change what's happened. But on occasions that aggression will not be forgotten, it will leave the ground with you and be carried along, a point best illustrated by JL from Ipswich.

I've never been one for trouble at football. It just isn't my thing and to be honest, I don't really understand it at all. But at the end of last season, after 10 years following Ipswich Town, I just snapped.

I was walking away from the ground after watching us lose out in the play-offs for the third season running and I was totally devastated. I still am. I mean, what else do we have to do? Anyway, I just wanted to get home, so I'd left my mates and headed for the car when this Bolton scarfer comes up to me and holds out his hand, all friendly like. I stopped and just told him to fuck off, which isn't like me at all, and he said something like, 'There's no need to be like that, it's only a game.' Well, it might only have been a game to him, but it was a fucking sight more than that to me and for some reason I just snapped. I don't know why, frustration, anger, who knows? But I turned round and really lumped him one. I was ashamed of myself straight away but I was bollocksed if I was going to apologise. I don't know what made me do it and I hope I never do it again. But I have to say, it sure as shit made me feel better.

While this illustrates how an individual can just snap at football and do things totally at odds with their normal behaviour, it also illustrates the essential difference between 'normal' fans and the hooligans. Because for the latter, taking those rivalries and passions out of the ground and beyond what most people would regard as acceptable is not only routine, it is an essential part of their match-day experience. For them, what happens off the pitch is as important as what happens on it, because they regard the reputation of the team and the fans as one and the same. If someone does something to affect that, be it a player or a rival mob, then they will try and redress the balance by exacting revenge in the only way they can. It is the fact that they overstep that boundary that marks them out as hooligans and what they do as hooliganism.

It is essential to recognise one point here: football hooligans are football fans. The media and the game may think otherwise, but that simply betrays how little they understand the nature of the problem. At the root of the hooligan issue is the game itself, and there is nothing to suggest that if any of these lads stopped going to matches they would cause similar trouble elsewhere. Indeed, most rivalries between particular hooligan groups or even individuals rarely, if ever, extend beyond match days. On the very few occasions that they do, it will inevitably involve something ridiculous like a group of lads on holiday, Sunday morning football or even another sport where there are links with specific football clubs. The prime example of that is boxing. Certain clubs, such as Birmingham, Cardiff, Millwall and L*t*n, have very close associations with individual fighters. When those fighters meet each other, it is often an opportunity for the rival football mobs to kick things off.

So what are the root causes of hooliganism? Why does football attract a sizeable minority of normally rational people who do not simply shake hands after a good game and have a beer and a laugh together but instead step over that line and adopt a movement which is, in effect, a sinister sub-culture akin to gang warfare? The academics have their theories about social deprivation, rebellion, etc, but to me, even if I gave them any credence (which I don't), these are excuses, not causes. No, as far as I am concerned, the vast majority of hooliganism as we know it today is caused by one of two things, which are interlinked: history and reputation. The history of a certain fixture or the reputation of a certain firm.

Mention any football club to anyone who either is or has been involved in hooliganism and they will instantly equate it to the reputation of their mob or a specific incident of trouble. A certain club in south-east London illustrates the point perfectly. If ever a club evoked instant thoughts of crowd violence, it is Millwall. Even today, 14 years on, I can readily conjure up images of their fans rampaging across the pitch at Kenilworth Road, hurling plastic seats before them. Those images formed, or rather enhanced, a reputation that has stuck with the club ever since, despite their best efforts to remove it. That has two key knock-on effects. The first is that many people outside the game, and a few within it, continue to think that hooliganism and Millwall are inseparable, which means that all Millwall fans, old or new, are immediately tainted. The second is that when Millwall – and the same applies to any club with a history of trouble – travel around the country, the police will be on the offensive and the locals will be either hiding or looking to have a pop to build up their own reputation. The losers are the decent, law-abiding members of the Millwall support who only want to watch a game of football and not be herded around like sheep or abused by rival fans whenever they travel away.

Conversely, if you take my own club Watford, which has become known as 'the family club', the idea of it being associated with any degree of football violence astonishes some people. When they come to Vicarage Road, visiting supporters do not expect to experience trouble. Nor do they when the Watford fans visit their ground and, in the main, they do not. Yet despite this image, the club has always had a small element of troublemakers among its support and in recent years that element has become increasingly violent. Eventually, through travelling around and fronting up more active firms at places such as Bristol City, the Watford firm's reputation will grow to the extent that when other clubs play Watford, their own firms will expect trouble and so will bring trouble when they come. And again, there will be a knock-on effect for everyone else at the club.

Of course, the ultimate example of a team with a bad history is England. A reputation formed on the streets of Luxembourg and Rimini continues to haunt England fans wherever they go, to such an extent that it actually becomes the cause of more problems. English supporters, as an entity, are still perceived as trouble abroad and are, more often than not, treated accordingly. But if you expect trouble and prepare for it in the manner that many countries do, you will inevitably get it. And while that is especially true of the authorities in other countries, as we saw during the 1998 World Cup, it is no less relevant to the plight of clubs such as Millwall in this country.

We should not forget, however, that if a group of fans have become saddled with a reputation, it will only be because it is richly deserved. Furthermore, there will be people who play up to that reputation and so, in effect, keep it going. And while certain groups may go through periods of inactivity, every so often they will explode back onto the scene and let everyone know they are still active. One of the most obvious examples of that came at Lansdowne Road, Dublin, in February 1995 when rioting England fans, fired up by the involvement of a few political extremists and exploiting some of the most inept organisation ever seen at a professional fixture, forced the abandonment of the Republic of Ireland versus England match. It reaffirmed the impression that England fans and trouble go hand in hand.

Another example of a club suddenly bursting back onto the scene with a vengeance came in February 1999 when Millwall, who had been reasonably quiet on their travels for most of the season, took a massive mob to Maine Road for their Second Division clash with Manchester City, who had been relegated the previous season. There was always going to be trouble at this fixture. Both clubs are well known for having active and violent hooligan followings and it was fairly obvious that each would want to establish themselves as better than the other. Yet very few people could have guessed quite how bad it was to become.

The build-up to the game had not gone well. In the encounter at the New Den the previous September, there had been numerous incidents involving the fans, including a massive pitch invasion during the match. The City manager Joe Royle even claimed his team had been victimised. Not only had a player been sent off, but Royle claimed that his striker Shaun Goater had been subjected to horrific racial abuse from the home fans. As the game in Manchester approached, Royle told the City faithful that his team would 'settle one or two old scores' at Maine Road, a statement that did not go down well with either the police or the Millwall board. Despite this, or maybe because of it, the Greater Manchester police turned down a request for increased capacity and security for the Millwall fans. It was clear that the mood on match day would be ugly, and so it proved.

Things started badly when Millwall supporters clashed with groups of both City and Manchester United fans at Stockport railway station. Running battles broke out which soon spilled over into adjoining streets before the police took hold of the situation. By lunchtime, Millwall had an estimated 1,500 lads in the centre of Manchester and more trouble erupted as the game approached. By kick-off time, the atmosphere in the ground was manic and when Paul Dickov scored for City in the second half, the Millwall fans charged at the North End, ripping out seats and hurling them at the home fans. Police in riot gear came in and baton-charged the Millwall fans, quickly restoring order, but the pattern had been set. Shortly before the final whistle, with City 3–0 up, the police announced that the Millwall fans would be kept in until the home crowd had dispersed. Twenty-five minutes later, the Millwall fans left Maine Road to find three of their coaches without windows and one of the drivers badly hurt after a gas canister had been thrown through a window. As police escorted a large group of them to

Piccadilly train station there was more trouble. Shop windows were put through and missiles thrown both from and at the group. Yet Millwall hadn't finished yet. Later that night, a group steamed down the so-called 'curry mile' in Rusholme and put through a number of restaurant windows before heading back to London. In all, 11 people were arrested, eight from Millwall, and nine police officers were hurt, one with a broken wrist. For a time, every cell in south Manchester contained supporters who had been detained as a result of trouble surrounding the game. It had been, according to an inspector from Greater Manchester police, 'a return to the dismal days of the past' and Millwall were once again dragged under the scornful gaze of both the media and the FA.

The reason this fixture generated these problems is, as I have already said, because of the history of both clubs' hooligan groups. Now, of course, as a result of what happened at this game, when the two teams next meet the rivalry between the fans will be rekindled, and so on ad infinitum. Each encounter simply adds a new chapter to the history.

Yet while hooligan firms having digs at each other is one of the more usual methods of firing up these rivalries, they can be started in any number of ways. Local derbies or even inter-county affairs such as Leeds–Manchester are some of the more traditional causes, but others are less obvious. What follows is one such example. It was sent to me by Martin, a Stoke City fan from Oldham.

In October 1995, we drew Newcastle in the Coca-Cola Cup at our place. We were really up for it and had lads out all over looking for their mob. Eventually we found out that they were drinking in a pub in Fenton but we couldn't really get near them as the police were all over us. In the end we gave up and went to the ground, but once we got there we heard that the sick Geordie bastards had beat the shit out of this young Stoke girl for no reason. As if that wasn't bad enough, they sliced her up as well.

Well, this spread through the lads like wildfire and after the game it was like World War Three. Stoke lads were attacking them from everywhere, from the ground right up to the train station. It was mental and I even heard that one of their buses got turned over onto its side. But I tell you this, if we ever play them again it'll be even worse. It's one thing having it away with lads, but picking on kids, well, that just ain't on.

Another way a feud can start is if a club or even a city experiences some kind of tragedy. If such a thing happens, it is, sadly, inevitable that at some point a group of rival fans will use it to upset or taunt their opposite numbers. Manchester United have suffered more than most from this as songs about the Munich air crash have been heard at many grounds over the years, while back in the late 70s and early 80s, Leeds United supporters were taunted with songs claiming that the Yorkshire Ripper, a notorious serial killer of the time, was beating the local prostitutes 12–0. Furthermore, Spurs fans were for many years subjected to groups of rival fans hissing at them (and if you don't know, I'm not going to explain it). Such taunting has never been one of the more attractive sides of fan behaviour yet it seems to be on the increase. In November 1998, Chelsea visited Leicester City, a club with whom they already had a long history of trouble, and their fans were subjected to a barrage of songs about their former and much loved director Matthew Harding, who had been killed in a helicopter crash. The Chelsea lads went mental and major trouble erupted outside the ground. Undoubtedly, certain elements among the supporters of both clubs will carry this on whenever the fixture list throws them together.

Another example involved, shamefully, my own club. In August 1998, Bradford City came to Vicarage Road. What follows was sent to me by one of their supporters, Simon H.

I do wonder sometimes about the mentality of some people. I mean, what kind of bloke thinks holding up a lighter and then dancing around pretending he's on fire is funny? I tell you what kind of person, shall I? A cunt. And as for the songs, well, let's just say I hope the lads with me managed to catch up with the twats who were singing.

I've been about a bit and at Bradford we've certainly had a fair share of problems, but there are some things you just don't do and one of them is take the piss out of things like that. I mean, 56 people died in that fire and some of them were friends and family. That isn't something you forget. We'd only ever heard it from three other clubs before and the last place we ever expected it was at Watford. I mean, aren't they the so-called family club? Some fucking family.

I know that some of the Bradford fans complained but from where I was, I couldn't see anything being done. All I can say is that your lads better keep a low profile when they come up here. If they don't, they'll pay for that.

* * *

Another way to wind up an opposing mob and spark off trouble is to taunt them about specific hooligan incidents. One of the best examples of this involves two clubs who are party to one of the most long-standing and violent rivalries in English football. Ironically, neither of them are English at all. They are, of course, Cardiff City and Swansea City. As most supporters will be aware, the history of confrontation involving these two sets of fans is long and bloody. Yet despite the many hundreds of incidents between them over the years, there is one in particular that has stuck in their collective memory: the swim-away story.

If you talk to followers of the two clubs, you will hear hundreds of different versions of this incident. Indeed, it now seems that there were actually two episodes. The first took place on a May Bank Holiday in the early 70s when some Swansea fans were attacked by a group of Cardiff supporters at Barry Island. But the second, and more important, took place in Swansea towards the end of the 80s.

The basic facts as I have uncovered them are these. Cardiff had travelled to Swansea and, as usual, were busy causing mayhem in the city centre. The Cardiff group the PVM (Pure Violence Mob) from Port Talbot were playing an active part in this but for some reason, about 10 of them had travelled independently of the main party and, rather than go into the city centre, had made their way down to the seafront. Unfortunately, they ran into a large Swansea mob and came under attack. Despite standing for a time, the PVM lads were forced to run into the sea to escape the Swansea fans and finished up standing chest-deep in the water. Rather than follow them in, the locals began bombarding them with rocks until the police came and rescued them.

Despite the Cardiff fans' assertion that this was only a minor defeat and had more to do with the numbers involved than the quality of their firm, the incident quickly settled into local folklore and even now, over a decade later, Swansea fans will taunt their Cardiff opponents by mimicking the front crawl. It usually has the desired effect.

It is stating the obvious but the one constant in all of the above is history, and the same can be said of almost every other incident of football violence that occurs. Football fans have long memories and hooligans even longer ones, and if something has happened in the past to fire up anger or rivalry between two sets of fans, inevitably one day someone will do something to exact revenge or exploit it. It could be as simple as walking round a corner and getting a slap from an irate Norwich fan or as frightening as walking onto a tube station teeming with West Ham. But if you are part of a mob and someone turns you over, you are duty bound to respond and gain recompense. This is why I firmly believe that history is the most important factor behind trouble at football and the tragedy is, it is all but impossible to deal with. You simply cannot change what has already happened.

Occasionally, however, past events, at least sporting ones, play no part in this issue at all. Sometimes the hooligans will not be guided by history, they will try and make it. What follows was sent to me by a good mate of mine who, although a Watford fan, has a sad affection for Hull City. It illustrates perfectly how crowds can, on occasions, have a massive effect on the future of their particular club.

It was the last game of the 98/99 season and

Swansea needed a win to guarantee a play-off place, although given that they had beaten Cambridge a few nights earlier, it would have taken a mathematical disaster for them to miss out.

Anyway, I had been told that because of a massive storm, there would be a pitch inspection before the game as the surface was swimming. But given the situation, it seemed almost impossible that it would be called off and so I confidently took my place outside the turnstile of the Hull City end.

Just about 3pm the game was called 'on' and the gates opened, which meant the kick-off would be delayed for a time. Panic then set in as I was told it was all-ticket and having travelled over from Bristol that morning on the off-chance I would see the game, I didn't have one. Fortunately, they had relaxed the ticketing arrangements at the final minute, as Hull could not go down and the expectation of a large away following had diminished. In fact, there were still several hundred Tigers milling around, but outside the Swansea entrances the roads were packed. In the end, I had a child's ticket shoved into my hand by someone with a spare, and after a moment of holding my breath as I walked through the turnstile, I ended up on the piss-poor excuse of a terrace.

Within a few minutes of opening the gates, the Swansea end was packed and immediately it was clear that the locals weren't taking anything for granted. The 'lads' congregate in the corner nearest to the away fans, and although there are a few advertising boards preventing fans from getting onto the pitch, at about 3.30 a roar went up and about three groups came on and ran towards the Hull contingent. Virtually every advertising hoarding was ripped up straight away and the triangle supports at the back of them were being thrown into the visitors' enclosure. A few Hull boys who were more than prepared to show their colours ran down to the front of the stand, but the barrage was forceful and swift and no one stood a chance. A couple of umbrellas were hurled like javelins into the Hull fans but after about 10 minutes, the police and stewards managed to clear the pitch of both people and debris and the game was near to starting.

So, as half-time happened everywhere else, the game in Swansea was just kicking off. That meant that, as every other game was finishing, the second half was about to start! Swansea had a distinct advantage of knowing exactly what they had to achieve, although the pressure was lifted when, after about half an hour, Swansea scored and the second big invasion occurred.

The whole thing seemed so contrived and to be honest, without wanting to credit the Swansea fans with any merit, they knew exactly what they were doing. The boys created a diversion, while other groups ran on from other directions. One guy spent the whole game baring his backside at the Hull City fans and as a result took the attention of both police and stewards. The invasions came from nowhere near this guy, even though the main congregation of yellow jackets were in the area of the 'lads'.

With about 20 minutes to go it was obvious this game was over. Halifax had lost, Swansea were there and at 2–0 up the game was over. All that remained was the inevitable third pitch invasion at the end of the game, this time with no foreseeable end to it, and many, many more people involved. Most of the Hull City fans wanted to leave, but were held in 'for your own safety'!

As the final whistle approached, I asked a steward if I could leave and showed her my Watford shirt, but she just accused me of stirring up all the trouble. After all, what was a Watford fan doing in the Hull enclosure? In the end, I was taken out across the front of the main stand in full view of the Swansea fans, who sussed that people were leaving rather too early.

I made it to my car and got the hell out moments before the final whistle and yet another pitch invasion. The thing that struck me most was that if the other results had gone against Swansea, meaning that they would have missed out on the play-offs, there was no way that game would have finished. Such was the atmosphere, the ref would have abandoned it without hesitation, leaving the final say in the hands of the FA. He seemed to be giving everything Swansea's way to such an extent that Hull fans thought he might as well have had a number 12 on his back. Thank Christ Hull didn't need a result, that's all I can say, because the whole thing was a bloody disgrace.

Although incidents of crowds genuinely affecting results are rare in this country, they do happen. In October 1997, Watford travelled to the home of the old enemy L*t*n and by half-time were 4–0 up. Such was our dominance it could actually have been many more, and would have been were it not for one important factor: the Watford goals were scored in front of the home fans. As each ball hit the back of the net, they became more and more agitated to the extent that after the game, the referee all but admitted that he had not given an obvious penalty to Watford because he feared that the locals would riot had he done so. As it was, by the time the players came out for the second half, mounted policemen had been forced to come onto the pitch in an attempt to calm things down. Thankfully, things settled down a little after that but for a while, many Watford fans at the game feared the home support would cause enough trouble to force it to be abandoned.

One reason trouble of this nature is on the increase in this country is because the clubs are now telling the fans to create it. Be it a cup tie, a play-off game or even an important league game, managers are now coming out and firing up the crowd in the local press. They call for an intimidating atmosphere and, as such, are asking for the crowd to be aggressive. But they know that generally speaking, the bulk of that aggression will come from the hooligan element and 'the lads', and it will manifest itself in abuse and hatred. To me, such requests border on incitement because while we all like a good, passionate atmosphere inside a ground, it inevitably has a knock-on effect off it. If a firm gets wound up, there is no way it will leave that mood behind as it walks out of the gate. Such appeals go unpunished, but the fact that they are made confirms that clubs know just how influential supporters can be.

The fear is that one day, a group of supporters in this country will pre-empt the request or even turn it on its head and, in return for the creation of atmosphere, make demands of the club they follow. To take that a few steps further, how would any club react if the leader of their main firm walked into the chairman's office and demanded free tickets or subsidised travel in return for not causing mayhem at a specific game?

In Italy, such things are the norm. The Ultras who follow the clubs there know they have power and frequently wield it, to such an extent that no one puts up a banner inside a ground without the permission of the leaders, or *capi*. In the past, the Ultras have used various tactics to register their displeasure at something, including turning their backs on the pitch at specific times or even watching games in complete silence. And on occasions, things get more sinister. Despite the fact that it is against the law to have any dealings with the Ultras, there have been many occasions when a club's refusal to supply tickets has resulted in crowd violence or serious vandalism. There have even been a number of cases of the Ultras influencing player selection and even dictating who the club should, or rather should not, buy. One famous example came three seasons ago when word spread among the fans at Verona that they were about to sign a black foreign international. Later that week, a dummy gallows was set up outside the ground and a black cardboard figure in a team shirt hung from it. Needless to say, the player was not signed.

Thankfully, we do not have such a situation in this country and many doubt we ever will. But at a time when the relationship between the English game and the fans is at an all-time low and the exploitation of supporters' loyalty shows no signs of abating, consider this: football sells itself on the back of a big-game atmosphere. How long will it be before some of the more volatile groups begin to think about what their role in the creation of that atmosphere is actually worth to the clubs? Personally, I don't think it's very far away at all because for the fans there would be a very obvious trade-off: tickets.

At the majority of clubs, getting tickets for home and

away games is a simple process. Season tickets take care of the home ones and if you need them for away games, you go down the club and hand over your hard-earned. In the Premiership, it isn't always that easy. Allocation by ballot seems to be on the increase especially at the big clubs, which, while fair up to a point, does nothing to reward loyalty. It also does nothing for you if you go to every game with 20 other lads, because the chances are many of you will not even get in, never mind you all sitting together. The clubs, of course, could not care less who gets the tickets just as long as someone pays – and neither do you, as long as you and your firm get yours. So, a few chosen words here, a threat or two there, and who knows what could be achieved? The hooligans already use violence against other clubs, so why not use it against their own? Especially when the club they love, or at least the people who work at it, think nothing of shafting them at every turn. And if it worked once, it would set an alarming and terrifying precedent (mind you, who's to say it hasn't already?).

If, or should that be when, football allows itself to get into this situation, then it will quickly find itself in real trouble. And this brings us back to my original point: football hooliganism exists because it *can*. And while the game allows it to exist, human nature dictates that the people involved will push their luck as far as they can, until someone decides to do something constructive to stop them. Until that issue is addressed, then we cannot be surprised at just how far the hooligans may be prepared to go.

Chapter 2
Who?

In the aftermath of the trouble involving England fans in Marseille during the 1998 World Cup, one of the most common media refrains was amazement that the people deported or detained in France had 'jobs and families'. The naiveté of this still astonishes me. Football hooligans do not live under stones and have 'THUG' tattooed across their foreheads. They are normal blokes who, in most cases, lead average, respectable lives. I have met many hundreds of people involved in hooliganism over the years, and with very few exceptions they are decent, friendly and above all 'normal' lads. If you actually bother to ask them why they have adopted this culture – something most people who 'study' the issue seem somewhat reluctant to do – many will simply shrug their shoulders; others will say, 'It's the buzz,' while a few will simply say, 'Why not?' None of which, of course, provides much of an answer.

But if you step back and think about it, this is yet another question which is being asked arse about face. Because the truth is that in most cases, people do not adopt the culture of hooliganism, it adopts them. You do not suddenly decide that going to football and causing trouble would be a good idea; you go to football first and it gradually sucks you in until you have become a part of the problem without even realising or acknowledging it. Once you're in, you're in, and it is very difficult to step back from that point without good reason, as I know from personal experience.

The main reason for that is because being involved in football violence is the most incredibly exciting and enjoyable thing. To anyone who has not been a part of it, that will probably be an astonishing statement but nevertheless, it is the truth. People who indulge in violence and intimidation at games do so because it allows them to experience extremes of every emotion known to man, on occasions within the space of 10 minutes. In this respect, as I have argued on numerous occasions, football hooliganism is the original extreme sport. Surely, if sports such as snowboarding and bungee jumping are about placing yourself at risk and over-coming your fears to experience elation and relief, it does not take a genius to work out that exactly the same thing applies to hooliganism. Hurtling down a slippery slope on a plank of polished wood could not possibly get the adrenaline pumping more vigorously than walking though the sidestreets of Cardiff with 10 or 20 lads on a match day. Anyone who has ever done that will know that it really does get the senses buzzing. Indeed, being involved in football violence actually has one distinct advantage over the uses of snowboarding if you are looking for excitement. Once you've hurtled down that slope on your plank a few times, the buzz you get from it diminishes and you're off looking for a longer, more slippery slope. But for the hooligans, every match day is different from the rest because each corner you turn could be *the* corner. As a result, the adrenaline rush never tails off and it is that buzz that is so attractive – you could even say addictive. You might not even have any kind of fight, you might even be running, but it's that buzz, a mixture of fear, anger, elation and anticipation, that gets hold of you. To a degree, this is one of the key elements of this debate because once you understand that, then you understand why the hooligans do what they do and it also explains why, once you've been involved, it never leaves you. Even now, over a decade since I was last in any trouble, I still jump up and watch when something happens rather than sitting down and shaking my head in disgust. But I am never alone, not by a long chalk. How many people can say that the sight of a ruck inside a ground doesn't get the blood racing? Someone once remarked to me that football violence made them feel alive, and I can understand exactly what they meant. So why on earth would anyone want to give it up?

But to return to our original question, how does an individual become involved and what is it that turns a normal, law-abiding lad into someone who will readily and happily indulge in violence under the banner of their chosen football club? There are many different ways it can happen but generally it all boils down to peer pressure, be it applied or imagined. What follows is one example that seems to be fairly typical of lads who were involved in the early to mid 80s. It was sent to me by Pat, a Chelsea fan exiled in Worcester.

As a child I always remember watching *Grandstand* or *World of Sport* when things kicked off at, say, Manchester United or Chelsea or wherever, and thinking, 'That must be great fun tearing up and down the pitch and nobody really appearing to get hurt.' Then I saw Leeds fans rioting on television at the Parc des Princes after being beaten by Bayern in the European Cup final. The following day at school, friends and I re-enacted the scene as if we were there.

I suppose I should give the broken home, inner-city slum, deprived childhood thing, but I can't, because it's simply not true. I had respectable parents, a good education and a very happy childhood. I have also never lived in a city, and could quite conceivably be considered a country bumpkin, although that's not how I see myself at all.

I supported Chelsea because they had a fashionable aura to them, and they had won the Cup-Winners' Cup in 1971. Unfortunately, we moved from Newbury to the West Midlands when I was 13, and moved to the most boring two-bit town in Britain, dubbed 'Sleepysville'. Fitting in was quite easy but being a small kid with a southern accent, I was picked on for the first few months, although I was always able to stand up for myself. Bullies are great for small kids to build a reputation off.

In my mid teens I hung round with a kid who had four older brothers, one of whom was a West Brom fan. While drinking in the local pubs, you could see them organising trips up the Albion and after a few weeks of the season had passed, me and my mates started going with them.

One of them used to organise cars and where to sit and drink, etc, and his personality was magnetic for me. He could really talk a great fight and we were all in awe of him, although we were later to find out that he could be very hot on his toes if he had to

be. The more we went to the Albion, the worse
the trouble became. It started with a bit of running
up and down the 'Brummie' Road, then moved on
very slowly until we were brawling at games most
Saturdays.

The day following a battle, we would meet up
and bask in the glory of it all, each thinking we were
really hard and giving out varying degrees of hero
worship to each other. I, for one, loved the attention
it brought me, showing off cut lips, black eyes and
chipped teeth as if they were medals.

Everything really changed in 1985, when all of
us sat in the pub one night and watched the documentary about the ICF. It was amazing and we
were all in awe of them. I mean, these guys were in
a different league to us. Then, a few months later,
West Ham came to the Hawthorns and so we all
went, not really to have a go, because I don't think
any of us was that confident, but more to see these
people. The events of the day seem unreal now but
they really did happen.

Some lads went by car but I travelled up by coach
to the ground. We were to meet up at the Blue Gates
pub, meaning that those of us on the coach had to
walk past the train station at Smethwick, which was
constantly emptying of West Ham fans. The police
escort did its job but there were thousands of them.
After having a couple of drinks (purely for medicinal
and nervous system purposes) we started for the
ground. As we left, one of the lads threw a beer mat
at me and I turned and jokingly said, 'Fuck off.'
The copper on the side of the road grabbed me
and started to walk me up the road, to my mates'
laughter and jeers. I thought he would bollock me

then let me go, but he started radioing for a van to take me away. At this I decided to do a runner and off I went, but to be honest, the copper made no real attempt to catch me.

When I got into my seat with the others, I noticed that the West Ham fans were in the upper tier behind us. This was the first time we had not been on the terraces because we wanted a close look at those ICF boys. Throughout the game West Ham pelted us with coins and gave us loads of abuse, which we gave back. My mate was arrested for giving the single-finger salute and this meant there was now a space in the car, which I duly decided to take.

After the game we followed the West Ham towards the island that goes across the motorway. Some West Ham were coming back the other way, walking back towards Birmingham, and as they passed through us one of them grabbed my arm and started giving me a bit of abuse but luckily, one of the others pulled me away and they just walked on.

When we got to the island we saw that the West Ham fans had stopped and one of them was walking around holding a Stanley knife and shouting in a broad Cockney accent, 'Come on, they want it, let's have it.' The next thing we know, they were steaming towards us but before I had time to run, I was hit full in the face and fell to the floor. I curled up like a little ball and waited for them to go but when I thought they had and rolled onto my back, someone stamped full on my face, breaking several of my teeth in the process.

When I got up, my mate's brother was slumped against some railings having just battled with a few of them. We started to make our way back to the car and wait for the others. Crossing back over the island we saw loads of Stanley blades and were counting ourselves quite lucky when some more of them came up and asked us the time. My mate said to ignore them and thankfully, they passed us by. I think they realised that having lost most of my teeth, I'd had enough for one day.

When we got back to the pub, we then went about building up the story for our mates. I was drinking my lager through a straw, partly because of the pain of the exposed nerves in my front teeth, but more for the effect of the tale. I probably learnt more that day about the way things work than any other. We thought we had been something but the ICF were a different class altogether. But the other thing I learnt was that I liked the attention. I suppose that's why I ended up a part of it for so long. Shortly after that, I started following Chelsea a lot more and trouble-wise, things got much worse.

As any male will known, the power your mates or fellow football fans can exert over you is immense. It is easy to tell a 13-year-old that he should walk away from trouble if it breaks out, but that isn't so simple for him if he's with a group of lads on an away trip and they suddenly become involved in a bit of mischief. Indeed, back in the 70s and 80s when hooliganism inside grounds was commonplace, if you had a lad who went to football on a regular basis with a load of mates, it was almost inevitable that one day, be it through fear, bravado or bottle, he would do something he shouldn't – because every lad knew that if he did anything which made him look bad or he let down his mates, it would live with him forever. Conversely, if he did something which made him look good, no one would ever forget it.

Most of us will be able to recall specific examples of this kind of thing quite easily. Whenever I see two certain lads at Watford, for example, I immediately, and subconsciously, recollect two incidents that happened many years ago. One where one of the lads concerned tried to do a runner from a ruck, and the other where the second lad walked out into a massive gap between us and a group of L*t*n on the terrace at Kenilworth Road and gave them the biggie. After all this time, I don't think any more or less of either of them, and I didn't back then, but I still do it. It's an instinctive and unavoidable thing.

Today the hooligans are less obvious than they were but it is still easy to become involved with a group who are loud and lairy, and for many people that in itself is an attraction. After all, part of the appeal of going to football for many of us is that it is very much a group activity. Going as a group brings different dimensions into the whole match-day experience, important and enjoyable aspects such as travel and pre-match pubs. If you went to a game on your own and started mouthing off, pretty soon you'd either be under arrest or under anaesthetic, but if you're with a group of lads such behaviour is more often than not expected of you. Not only that but, as well as being a bloody good laugh, being a part of a group gives you a feeling of anonymity which encourages you to be abusive and, in the case of some people, violent; to act in a manner that is totally at odds with the way you would behave in the comfort of your own home. You can, in effect, leave behind your middle-class, family values and dumb down to the working-class, right-wing stereotypes so beloved of the media and our academic friends. Proof of this can be found in any firm in the land because to an outsider, most of the lads involved will come across as being from exactly the same mould. They sound the same, act the same and may even wear the same clothes. But more often than not, away from football, their backgrounds are fantastically diverse. I am constantly amazed by the types of people I meet who are or have been involved in hooliganism: doctors, solicitors, bankers, factory workers, journalists, policemen, firemen, company directors, taxi drivers, etc. I have seen all these esteemed occupations represented among the hooligan world over the years and have heard of an awful lot more. There have even been very strong rumours circulating on the hooligan grapevine that a number of 'celebrities' have been involved in trouble in recent years. These include one very well-known pop star who has allegedly not only been involved with a particular firm but has also occasionally funded their activities.

If true, it illustrates perfectly the fact that belonging to a group or gang is something that many people like to do and football provides them with the perfect and possibly only excuse. What is more, football firms do have a certain mystique about them which gives them a peculiar kind of fascination to people on the outside. This would certainly explain the allure such groups hold for those celebrities who like to be thought of as 'lads' and who have frequently been seen in the company of known hooligans.

Yet for many people, the real attraction of being a part of a firm is that it allows them to adopt a kind of schizophrenic and secret life, something which only they and the other members of the group know about. Indeed, in many cases the only relationship of any kind the members of the group will have with each other is through football, not even seeing each other as mates. When I was 'at it', no one at any of the units I was serving with had any idea of the things I was getting up to. Of course, I did everything I could to cover my tracks, such as those tales of car crashes and muggings on the occasions where I had been turned over. It wasn't just that as a serviceman I could not afford to have anyone find out, it was that I didn't want them to. What I did away from the unit was mine and had nothing to do with them (though I doubt the Military Police would have seen it quite that way had I been caught). I have heard similar tales from many people over the years and it has always intrigued me.

This is perhaps one of the reasons why so many firms assign themselves nicknames or tags. Once you have a name, then the group becomes an entity which in turn gives the individuals concerned a more solid identity and forges a camaraderie among them. Having the fact that you are a well-known member of a group such as the Central Element on your CV might not do you any favours at work, but among the footballing fraternity it will certainly attract a level of respect and, to be honest, fear. For this is another aspect of hooliganism which many people find appealing; the fact that it is, in effect, bullying. Exerting fear upon people can be an awfully powerful feeling. We all like to feel better, stronger and more powerful than the next man.

While most people, even outside football, have heard of the ICF and the Headhunters, groups such as the Five-0, the Soul Crew or the Naughty Forty are every bit as dangerous and, to the hooligans themselves, every bit as famous. Over the last few years, I have tried to piece together what I believe is the definitive listing of these firms, which can be found in an appendix at the back of this book. This has been an incredibly difficult and time-consuming process and I have relied on many people for help and information. The difficulty, of course, has been in separating fact from fiction. Some of the names that have been brought to my attention are so ridiculous that I still wonder if they are not the figment of someone's over-active imagination. Therefore, I have only included in the list names that I have been able to confirm through at least two separate sources, or which I was already aware of. I must stress that not all of these groups still exist. Some were consigned to history long ago, although it is reasonable to assume that many of the groups will simply have adopted new tags even though they have pretty much the same membership (this is a fairly routine tactic to either throw off the attentions of the Old Bill or to re-emerge after a particularly serious and humiliating hammering). Others have simply been swallowed up and incorporated into other firms, while a few – but not many – have been smashed by the activities of the boys in blue. In addition, it is almost certain that others will have been formed since this book went to press, for new firms seem to be springing up all the time.

It is also important to understand that some clubs have more than one active firm attached to them, although this phenomenon was much more prevalent in the early 80s than it is today. One of the main reasons for it was simply that with some of the larger clubs having support from different areas, groups of lads banded together with their mates rather than as a whole. As I have said, my own club Watford provided a good example of this. We had no real firm as such, but there were a number of little cliques of lads all of whom were game. We all knew each other by sight, but rarely, if ever, travelled together, let alone fought together.

Another thing to note is that not every hooligan is, or wants to be, a part of any kind of firm, be it organised or otherwise. What is more, some clubs simply do not have any kind of 'named' firm attached to them at all, as far as I am aware. But that does not mean that clubs such as Gillingham, Bournemouth or Wycombe, who do not feature on this list, do not have a violent element, far from it. What it might mean is that they are either inactive or simply fragmented.

In a similar vein, not every 'member' of a firm is a hooligan. If you look at a club such as Birmingham City, a good proportion of their supporters think of themselves as a part of the entity called the Zulu Army, because it is a label that most of their fans will happily attach to themselves. Yet while the club has a large and very active group of hooligans who also call themselves the Zulu Army, the bulk of the Blues' support would no more think of themselves as being party to football violence than my mum. Much the same thing can be said of Arsenal and the Gooners tag and, to a lesser extent, Chelsea and the notorious Headhunters. Many people, including a good number of former and active hooligans, deny that this last group ever really existed at all. Yet the name has become synonymous with both the club and football violence.

It also has to be recognised that not all these firms are organised, at least not in any sense the media would have the public believe. Many are simply loose groups of lads for whom any organising that takes place simply revolves around working out how you will travel and where you will drink. For others, it means ensuring that if the firm needs numbers for a specific game, people are contacted to make sure the mob has a full compliment and everyone knows what is expected of them. For the final group, the real players, organisation means just that: sorting out routes, pre-planning confrontations well away from the grounds or spotting for rival groups on match days. The reality, of course, is that this latter group of hooligan firms forms a very small part of the problem yet their influence is immense. It is, after all, their continued existence which spreads the most fear among the police and the authorities.

But one thing we should remember: every firm has members who will happily indulge in violence should the opportunity arise. There may be 2,000 of them, there may only be 20, but if you walk round a corner and there they are, the harm they can cause and the damage they can do is immense. And when you're lying by the side of the road battered and bruised, it doesn't matter one iota who did it. It still hurts exactly the same.

For every name linked to every firm, there is, of course, a story. Names just do not appear, they are deliberated upon and based around certain events, places or even characteristics. Portsmouth's 657 Crew, for example, are known for taking the early train to away trips: the 6.57. Another club with an interesting history is one which people do not immediately associate with hooliganism, Norwich City. As you can see from the appendix, they have had a number of firms over the years and the history of some of them was supplied to me by someone best known as East End NCFC. When I first read this, I immediately disregarded it as pure bullshit, but having met the geezer concerned, I am assured by him that it is absolutely genuine.

First firm I really knew, and swept me along, was The Steins, circa 1981, inextricably linked with Norwich's Magnificent Seven Scooter Club. I remember going to Ipshit Town the day after Boxing Day 1982 and never knowing anything like it. Toe-to-toe in the streets before the game, all over the ground, and more of the same after, all to the accompaniment of, 'Ipswich, wherever you may be, we are the mental Stein army.' At the return match in April, City broke into Carrow Road pre-match and painted 'Steins R Go' at the back of the River End. This was quickly taken up and appeared on walls all over Norwich the following summer. To this day, it can still be seen here and there!

I had a mate at the time who was a couple of years older than me and followed Spurs. I went to the 1981 Charity Shield with him and it was like a whole new ball game. Never mind the rows, exciting and terrifying though they were, all these exotic football fans in diamond Pringle jumpers and Lacoste rollnecks enthralled me, and 'casual' took over my teenage years.

This was before casual took off everywhere. In Norwich, by the summer of '83, everyone's kid brother was dressed up to the nines in Fila, Tacchini, Ellesse and Pringle, and dodgy Greeks were selling moody gear out of transit vans on Saturday afternoons that summer.

The few of us that were doing it prior to this were in small groups. Names, as I recall, were C Squad and C Firm (these drank in adjacent pubs both beginning with the letter C; C Squad were casuals, C Firm were skinheads), the Little Chefs (so called because of an incident once in a Little Chef – I wasn't there!) and the Trawlermen, from Great Yarmouth.

The City boys used to go to Hemsby, next to Great Yarmouth, nearly every weekend in the summers of '83 and '84 and every, yes, every weekend would end up with a massive row at Hemsby's Star Rooms.

In hindsight, the Trawlermen were more late 70s

and early 80s. I should elaborate on them, although I never really knew any of them – they were always a bit aloof. In fact, I suspect many of them were economic migrants who weren't really City supporters but liked a row. They weren't the most conspicuous mob around, but they hid from no one. They were much older than us at the time and were all dockers, oil rig workers and, yes, fishermen! They used to play up, at least that's what I hope it was, by wearing yellow oilskins to the game, sometimes even with those ridiculous yellow hats, too. Rumour had it that they occasionally used a complicated series of fishing nets to trap opposition supporters walking under a rail bridge – I must admit to never having witnessed that. Eerily, once in a while, for a big match, one of these oilskins from the past can sometimes be glimpsed.

Another example of how names come about was sent to me by CB from Bristol Rovers.

All Rovers fans are now known as Gasheads. It's not a specific crew connected with Rovers, we are just collectively known as The Gas.

The nickname, oddly enough, came courtesy of The Shit. It goes back to our Eastville days, where a large gasworks was situated next to the ground. The stadium was often engulfed in the spray that came from the cooling towers. The spray settled everywhere and had a distinctive odour about it; it permeated your hair, your clothes and even your skin, it was a wonderful smell which is now sadly missed. The Shit dubbed us dirty, smelly, stinking Gasheads. A prelude to a good rumble in a city centre pub would often be, 'Can you smell stinking gas in here?' followed by sniff, sniff. It was as predictable as 'Got the time, mate?'

With the decline of Eastville and therefore the decline of the Tote End, the Rovers fans needed a new identity. It came unwittingly from our dreaded enemy. We turned the insult of 'stinking Gashead' on its head and proudly adopted it as our new nickname. We are now as well-known as 'The Gas' as we are as 'The Pirates'.

There is, of course, much more to being a part of a hooligan firm than simply being a part of a gang. Irrespective of their standing in the hooligan world, there has always been a loose but distinct hierarchy in each and every group. It is inevitable that someone will come forward and take the lead and often, within a small mob of lads, he will be the one who is the most mouthy, the best fighter, or even the one who remains calm in any given situation. But within the long established and larger firms, the make-up will often be more structured.

As time passes, real leaders will emerge from among the ranks and they will be the people the police refer to as the 'King-Pins', but who are more generally known by such titles as 'Top Boys' or even 'Generals'. These men may well be public enemy number one as far as the FA are concerned, but they will be highly respected by the other members of the group, and often by their peers as well. Alongside them will be the lads who will always stand and fight, or who will even initiate or plan trouble. These tend to form what are commonly known as the hard-core or main firm. Behind them will come, in effect, the majority: people who will happily indulge in trouble if the numbers are right or things are in their favour but who will, nevertheless, always consider themselves as an important part of their specific firm or mob. The final group are the hangers-on. People who have no intention of becoming involved in any actual violence, but who will still shout the odds when they have numbers on their side. The size, and status, of each and every firm is wholly dependent on the respective size of each of these elements.

There is also a certain code of honour among the firms, one which draws specific boundaries marking what is and is not acceptable behaviour. For example, if you and your lads receive a battering at the hands of a rival mob, you do not go the police and complain about it, you simply exact revenge next time around. That's the way it works. But for many of the individuals involved, the fact that these boundaries are in place seems to subconsciously reinforce the belief that hooliganism is nothing more than a game. Violence for the sake of it might not be attractive, but kicking things off with another group of hooligans who also adhere to the rules is not looked down upon in quite the same way, either by those who inflict it or those who suffer as a result. Furthermore, many of those involved simply do not consider what they do to be wrong in any legal sense, because to a large extent among football fans hooliganism has never really been criminalised.

A simple comparison can be made with drink-driving. Most of us have either done it at one time or know someone who has, and we all know that it's against the law. Yet if we see someone leaving the pub who is clearly over the limit, do we shop them? No, we don't, because drink-driving still isn't regarded as a 'proper' crime and if the bloke gets caught, we think of him as being unlucky. Yet if he runs someone over, we quite rightly condemn him out of hand because then, he really has broken a law that everyone would regard as 'proper'. Hooliganism is exactly the same. For many, that isn't a 'proper' crime either. If we know who the people involved are, do we shop them? Almost certainly not, we more likely just think of them as 'lads'. Yet in reality, football hooliganism is nothing more than violent, pre-meditated crime, but because of this apathy towards it from many football fans, the people involved carry on their activities pretty much unmolested and are able to justify their behaviour to themselves because no one else seems to care. For some people, it is actually the getting away with it that is the main attraction. Only when they end up in court, and the anonymity they have enjoyed is removed, does the full realisation – and consequences – of what they have been doing, as well as risking, hit home. The sad reality, however, is that very few of the people involved in hooliganism will ever end up in court. They will simply carry on until they drift out of direct involvement after a few years because of age or boredom.

Having said that, hooliganism should never be thought of as a young man's game. Yes, there are plenty of young lads who run around a lot, get loud and cause problems. But there are plenty more who are in their late 20s, 30s or even 40s, and they are often more dangerous. Not only are they far more difficult for the police to deal with, because they know what's what with regard to the law, but as they are older, they are also less prone, or able, to run. With years of street-fighting experience behind them, they are often very violent indeed.

Two good examples of that were brought to my attention recently. The first was in July 1999, when the police announced that the average age of eight men being sent for trial following violent disorder at a Bury versus

Stockport game was 31. The second came from someone who had suffered the misfortune to stumble across a group of Millwall fans somewhere up north. Only 19 himself, he said simply that when things had kicked off, many of his firm, who themselves were no mugs, had bottled it because they simply could not fight with blokes who were older than their dads.

Even when people eventually drift out of week-to-week involvement, the majority of them may well still turn out for big games and will always think of themselves as a part of their particular firm. Some of them may even settle into legend. Among the hooligan fraternity are legions of names who are as much a part of English football's history as Bobby Moore or Jimmy Greaves, and they are held in very high regard by their peers.

Yet it is the fact that the whole thing continues almost unopposed, and certainly uncriticised, that reinforces the whole Saturday scene and lends it a kind of legitimacy. The result of that is that new people are drawn in – and the vicious circle continues unbroken.

PART TWO
The History

Chapter 3

The Early Years

When in August 1999, Cardiff and Millwall kicked off the new season in their own inimitable style, much was made of the 'shock' revelation that football hooligans were not only planning their activities using mobile phones, they were talking about it on the Internet as well! Quite why this use of new technology should have been of surprise to anyone baffles me. For if you look back at the ways in which hooligans have conducted their activities over the years, it is clear that they, as an entity rather than as individuals, have always taken the lead in their particular competition with the police. The law, after all, can only react, be it on the ground or through the courts. And no matter what legislation is brought in or what action is taken, the hooligans will always find a way round it in the end. Being one step ahead is an integral part of their game.

The evolution of hooliganism is one of the most fascinating aspects of the modern game. Just as the kind of football we see in the Premier League is very different to the game our dads watched in the 1950s, so the nature of crowd trouble we suffer today is totally different from the violence we experienced in the early 70s. Not in the sense of the actual physical act of combat – I would imagine a kick up the arse in 1972 wasn't that different from the one you would get today – but in the execution of that violence.

I have gone back much further than that to try to piece together a history of how hooliganism developed, and what the main influences on it have been. This account does not claim to be definitive, just as near to the facts as I have been able to get. To me, what I found was astonishing.

Violence involving spectators at football games is nothing new. In fact, although the game in its modern form began in the 1840s, incidents actually pre-date that by almost 500 years. The mediaeval version of football, where participants tried to move a leather-bound bladder between defended areas, was so violent that in 1365, Edward III actually banned it because he feared that the rivalries being stirred up would lead to civil unrest. Almost 300 years later, Oliver Cromwell was forced to take a similar step when he banned the game in the Midlands. Even back then, the Brummies were revolting.

By the time the game we know and love was delivered to a hungry public in the mid 19th century, trouble involving supporters was fairly commonplace. The recording of such incidents in the media was certainly becoming more frequent, although most did not involve actual violence but instead centred on simple abusing or even pickpocketing. The nature of any trouble was, in any case, completely different from the type of thing we began to see in the mid 1960s. Travel was extremely difficult, even for the players never mind the supporters, and so in most cases there were not many away fans except for games against fairly local clubs. Furthermore, while the FA was founded in 1863, the Football League did not come into existence until 1888. Up to that point, the structure of the game was fairly informal and many of the teams which grew into professional clubs were still playing on park land. Indeed, one of the earliest examples of crowd trouble I have been able to study arose in just such a situation.

On 30 September 1882, the Hotspurs cricket club, formed by two groups of schoolboys from north London, began playing competitive football matches on Tottenham Marshes. As they became more successful, they drew increasingly large crowds but, unfortunately, also attracted the attentions of the local youths, who became intent on causing trouble as the games were being played. On at least one occasion, the players had to defend the pitch from invasion and eventually were forced to employ the services of an adult to run the club and keep the local kids away. By 1887, the club had changed its name to Tottenham Hotspurs and were attracting crowds of up to 4,000 people – this on what was still a municipal park pitch with only a rope separating the crowd from the playing surface. Things really came to a head when an element of the crowd began stealing vegetables from nearby allotments and throwing them at visiting players. The FA were never involved but the local population, who were getting increasingly pissed off with their food supplies being raided, certainly were. As a result, the club were forced to move from the marshes and after various homes and even more trouble (including an incident where three L*t*n T*wn players were attacked) they ended up at White Hart Lane in 1899.

The example provided by events at Spurs was nothing unusual. In the period leading right up to World War One, the professional game was widely associated with crowd trouble. Local and often violent rivalries became more common, as did pitch invasions, which were usually designed to stop games where the home team was losing. On a number of occasions, supporters simply walked on to the pitch at half-time and refused to leave, forcing the game to be abandoned. Another problem was the number of attacks on players and referees, something which the FA were becoming increasingly concerned about. Figures available suggest that in the period between 1894 and 1914, there were 238 major incidents of crowd trouble at matches reported to the FA by referees. It seems likely that this was the tip of a very large iceberg, because it does not include any problems outside the grounds, or violence that the referees did not report.

Incidents declined sharply during World War One and the level of violence remained fairly low until the end of World War Two. However, there was still trouble around and often there were some very ugly occurrences indeed. Millwall, for example, suffered four ground closures between 1934 and 1950, the last one as a result of a 200-strong mob attacking a referee after a game against Exeter City.

The post-war years were a boom time for football in general. Crowds reached a peak in 1948–49 when more than 41 million went to a game. More and more women began attending matches, and crowd control continued to be carried out by small numbers of officers. There were occasional flare-ups between rival groups, of course, and some of those were very violent, but in the main what trouble there was involved small numbers and not much actual violence. Generally speaking, problems still centred around players, referees and drink. All that began to change in the mid 1950s.

In the post-war years, Britain's self-esteem began to go into sharp decline. The euphoria of victory in Europe was fading while the Empire was beginning to break up, as more and more nations strove for independence and a new beginning. At home, the economic boom most people had expected didn't materialise and as if that wasn't bad enough, in 1956 the country was drawn into an ill-judged and humiliating conflict in Suez. By 1957, the press had begun to express grave concerns about the problems being caused by an increasingly frustrated youth, some of whom were now causing problems at football. This drew increasing coverage in the papers as sports reporters began to include trouble inside grounds in their match reports. It was within such reports that the widespread use of a term that was to become synonymous with football violence first began. Originally used in the early 1920s, the label had originated from an Irish immigrant family who had terrorised the East End of London in the 19th century. The name Hooligan – or Houlihan – depending on where you research – had settled into history.

The rock and roll explosion of the 1950s has been blamed for many things ranging from rebellion to anarchy. One indisputable fact is that out of it came the Teddy Boys. For the first time, the youth had a culture of their own and although it was best characterised by dress, haircuts and music, it was just as well known for violence. The effect the Teddy Boys had on football was immense. Large numbers of them attended games actively looking for trouble and the movement was wholly to blame for a significant increase of crowd problems at games in the late 50s and early 60s. Pitch invasions became routine and were often accompanied by confrontations between rival fans. The anarchic attitude of the Teddy Boy movement caused serious problems more generally for the police, who, particularly in London, struggled to cope. No longer would the sight of a single copper be enough to calm a situation; often it would take the involvement of a large number of officers. The wholesale destruction of property also became a serious problem, trains being a particular favourite as the fans began to travel more freely.

By the time the cult of the Teddy Boys had begun to die down, to be replaced by the Mods and Rockers movements, the amount of violence at football, although alarmingly high compared to a decade before, had levelled off. Yet the problems caused by the Mods and Rockers, largely at seaside towns on Bank Holidays, but also at dance halls up and down the country, led the media increasingly to link their activities to those of the football fans on a Saturday afternoon. Looking back at it now, it seems to me that this link was not actually that strong; both groups were far more interested in bikes and music (and also, in the case of the Mods, clothes) than they were in football. But largely as a result of this misinformed media coverage, copycat gangs of football fans began to spring up all over the country. Slowly, trouble began to spread and from this point on, everything began to change.

Oddly, one of the most significant events in the growth of hooliganism seems to have been the televising of the 1962 World Cup in Chile. For almost the first time, English football fans were able to witness first-hand exactly how other countries' supporters got behind their teams. The singing, in particular, was a revelation and highlighted the fact that fans could play a more active role. Within weeks, supporters up and down the country had formed groups of their own. More importantly, they had begun to congregate in specific areas of their home grounds and claim them as their own. These were almost always behind the goal, which is how the concept of 'ends' as we know it today was born. They became *the* place to be on match days, not just for the singing but also for the humour. And with fans finally able to contribute to the occasion, the whole nature of supporting changed.

With many young men wanting to be a part of this new breed of football fan, the home ends at most grounds were packed solid. Because, on the whole, they were good-natured places, initially trouble was rare. Segregation was all but nonexistent at that time, largely because it wasn't really required, but from within the singing groups sprang an element who were 'leaders' rather than 'followers' and it is easy to see why the ends became an obvious target for rival fans later on.

Nineteen sixty-three was a significant year not just for football but for young British men in general. It was the year that marked the end of national service. I cannot imagine how much of a relief that must have been to anyone facing compulsory time in the Army, but this ending of conscription marked a major change in British society. Suddenly, the old values of respect, compassion and humility seemed to be less important. For the youth, the last link with the old way had been removed and rebellion was in the air. Nowhere was that more visible than at football. With money in their pockets and cheaper, faster and more reliable transport increasingly accessible, there was a sharp increase in the numbers of travelling supporters. Suddenly, gangs of football fans were travelling and causing trouble wherever they went. In November that year, Everton became the first club to erect fences behind the goals. Yet despite the rising amount of violence among the fans, the average English crowd was still largely regarded as being decent and law-abiding.

So much so that in October 1965, *The Times*, in common with a number of other papers, suggested that English clubs be withdrawn from European competition until the continentals had sorted out their own crowds' behaviour. Those words were to come back to haunt them within days. First, trouble erupted at both Old Trafford and at Huddersfield and then, a few weeks later, a notorious incident took place at Brentford.

Since their formation in 1885, Millwall FC had forged for themselves a reputation as a rough club with an even rougher set of supporters. By 1965 that reputation was firmly entrenched and Cold Blow Lane, a name which still sends shivers down the spine of many a football fan, had already become a no-go area unless you were either from Millwall, actually playing or simply insane. On their travels, especially around the other London clubs, the Millwall fans were fearless. But when they travelled to Griffin Park on 6 November, their actions were to have a major effect on the future of the game.

I have talked to many people about this match and have also read numerous reports, many of which contradict each other. Indeed, if everyone who claimed to be at Griffin Park on that day actually was there, then it must be a damn sight bigger than I remember! However, the simple facts are these; at some point during the game a hand grenade emerged from the terrace holding the Millwall fans and bounced onto the pitch. The fact that it was a dud is immaterial and was certainly not known by the players, who must have shat themselves. The papers went ballistic and with the World Cup due to be staged in England the very next year, they suddenly altered the way they were reporting upon the behaviour of supporters.

Initially, the press began to panic about problems in

the coming summer and although these failed to materialise, possibly because of the fears generated by the media, the pattern was set. From then on, coverage was given not just to incidents inside grounds, but outside as well. Back then, like now, football violence sold papers and as a result, reports and photographs became even more dramatic and headlines more sensationalist. This generated the impression that every game was accompanied by mayhem, something which was simply not the case. While trouble did occur at some games, in most cases it was simply groups of lads running around making lots of noise rather than actually hitting anyone, and most games passed off without anything happening at all. But the downward spiral had begun. And with football seemingly unable, or unwilling, to deal with the problem, it was only a matter of time before things got worse.

One thing no one seemed to realise at the time was that while crowds for domestic games were in sharp long-term decline, not just because of trouble but for various reasons including the fact that television was becoming more widely available, the number of so-called hooligans was remaining fairly constant. Therefore, in percentage terms, the hooligan element in the crowd was actually increasing.

So far, most incidents of football hooliganism had involved clubs that were fairly local to each other. Travelling long distances was still fairly arduous by train and for many supporters from the northern clubs, visits to London were 24-hour affairs, not by design as they are now but by necessity. If you went by car – that was if you even had a car – anything over 100 miles was a major expedition. Yet increasingly, fans were making the effort and among them were a significant number who were on the lookout for what the papers at the time termed 'bovver'. Each week the terraces would be alive with talk about who went where, who did what and what the visiting team would bring with them. Yet the truth was that no club, with the possible exception of Millwall at Brentford, had ever really done anything that we would consider today to be out of the ordinary. There had been plenty of running battles, of course, but nothing which really had the papers foaming at the mouth. That changed in May 1967, when an incident took place which took hooliganism onto a new level.

The clubs with the most notorious followers in 1967 were Millwall, West Ham and Chelsea. That they were all from London should not have surprised anyone, given that they had more local derbies and therefore more opportunity for violence, as well as easier travel. But the club with the largest support in the country was Manchester United. Even back then, they had a huge fan base in the south and every time the team came to London, they attracted massive crowds. Generally, the fact that there were so many of them meant that trouble was minimal because they simply swamped the grounds as well as the surrounding areas. They came to West Ham at the end of the 1966–67 season needing to win to secure the championship and brought thousands upon thousands of fans, who quite simply invaded East London. Fighting broke out early on as the West Ham fans, feeling somewhat put out, tried to regain some of their lost pride. United won the game 6–1 and therefore took the championship, but the day was far from over. As the crowd came streaming out of Upton Park, the celebrations began but more trouble erupted and the United fans simply began to trash the surrounding area. It was many hours before calm was restored but for the West Ham fans, it had been a crushing and humiliating day. Word of this invasion spread through the terrace grapevine and suddenly, United were being held up as the 'worst' firm in the country. In the eyes of some, they held that position for the next 10 years, including the 1974–75 season, when they spent a year in the Second Division, and their fans were involved in serious trouble at almost every game they played. The Cockney Reds, in particular, obtained a reputation for fearless and frequent violence, much of which took place at Euston station or on the London underground.

For the West Ham supporters, this episode forced a major change in their behaviour. From then on, they became even more violent than they had been and, significantly, they also began to travel more. The East End invasion also prompted supporters up and down the country to try to enhance their own particular reputations. Liverpool, Leeds, Portsmouth and even smaller clubs such as Aldershot experienced serious trouble in and around the grounds on a weekly basis. And it was all being made easier by the growing use of 'football specials'. Originally, clubs had used coaches to drive players to grounds, but as the distances increased and the demand from families and friends became more pressing, they began to hire carriages and use the railways. When the numbers of supporters wanting to travel also increased, the clubs took to hiring whole trains. Initially, these 'football specials' were simply methods of transport, but over the years they were to evolve into something which many people regard as one of the highlights of their supporting lives. The fact that the railways used old rolling stock was, in the main, immaterial. They were cheap and they moved, that was all anyone needed or wanted.

Ironically, the specials were at first seen as a godsend to the police, for they allowed them to exercise strict controls over the movement of supporters around the country. Yet that had little effect on the activities of the supporters because they were still not segregated inside grounds. Visiting groups had begun to go into home ends to try to kick things off and the areas around grounds frequently experienced some very violent confrontations, often involving significant numbers of people. Now, from within those groups, emerged a specific but very loose kind of hierarchy. The London clubs, in particular, were well known for having leaders who called the shots whenever anything happened, and in their own way they became as famous (or infamous) among the supporters as any of the players.

As media interest in the activities of the hooligans grew and crowds continued to decline at an alarming rate, the image of the game seemed to take a battering week in, week out. It must have been difficult back then to imagine how things could get any worse for football, yet this was only the beginning. For in the late 1960s, a new element was to enter the equation: the skinheads.

Much has been written about the skinhead culture and today most people will have a specific and unpleasant image of exactly what skinheads were. However, the reality is somewhat different. Skinhead culture was about three things: music, clothes and football, and the one thing the original skinheads were not was racist. After all, ska and reggae, which was and remained their favoured music, originated in Jamaica and was brought to Britain by immigrants in around 1968. Indeed, there were plenty of Afro-Caribbean skins around at the time, although it has to be said that both black and white skins were less than friendly towards the growing Asian community. Sadly, right-wing politics was to infect and all but consume the scene later on. But as 1969, the golden year for skinheads, came and went, football became a natural environment for all those who were into the scene, driven as it was by working-class roots and a fierce loyalty to their community.

The skinhead influence on football was major. As the game moved into the 1970s, almost every club in the country had a mob of sorts. Some, such as Leeds, Man United and the big four London clubs, were massive. Worryingly for the police, football violence was also becoming fashionable. The anarchic approach to life and the dressing-up which typified the skinhead movement captured the imagination of the tabloids and soon their activities were receiving even more coverage than before. By this time, groups were actively seeking publicity. The Sunday papers would be devoured religiously for stories of trouble and many a teenager had a scrapbook under his bed detailing exploits of violence among rival fans. If you could actually make the paper yourself, your status went through the roof.

It was around the same time that the 'taking' of ends became widespread. It had always gone on, of course, but now it became a thing of honour not only to take an end but to protect your own. There were various ways this was done but at many grounds, visiting fans could simply walk around the perimeter until they came to the home end. If they got in early, they would already be waiting when the locals came in, but if they got there late, it was simply a matter of fronting them up until something happened – which it invariably did. The first visible sign of this was usually the opening up of a large, gaping hole on the terrace. Around the edges would stand the rival groups and every so often one would rush forward, lashing out with boots or fists, before being pushed or pulled back. Within a minute or so, the other group would respond and attack in the same manner. It sounds daft now, but often it was incredibly violent and once things had kicked off, it usually took a concerted police action to sort things out and get the groups apart. Taking someone's end in the early 70s was the ultimate result for visiting mobs as it proved that you were better than they were, and the sheer visible drama of a terrace battle attracted even more press coverage. It was the very last thing the game needed.

By now, the skinheads were firmly entrenched on the terraces of many clubs, though they were not the only groups causing trouble at games. Not everyone was or wanted to be a skinhead. What follows is an extract of a letter sent to me by lifelong Bristol Rovers fanatic Chris B.

Back in the wonderful, dreamy era of the 70s, pre-designer gear and mobile phones, football mobs (most of them, at any rate) did not really have specific tribal names. But most football hoolies congregated on the traditional covered ends, so consequently they just took their name from that part of the ground. Therefore BCFC (the Shit) were the East End, Arsenal the North Bank, and so on. Rovers took their name from that part of the ground where you could also place a bet, due to the fact that the stadium also held greyhound racing events (the front of the roof carried huge timing clocks). Consequently we became the Tote End, or simply the Tote.

The Tote End certainly dominated Bristol football from the late 60s to the early 70s and it was a fearsome place. The odd thing about Rovers fans back then was that there was quite a mix, a real melting pot of teenage cultures. Sure, the majority were skinheads (as I was) but there were also a large proportion of bikers, or Greebos as they were commonly known. This, I think, was very rare at most football stadiums – certainly the Shit had no such equivalent – but this melting pot led to a unique atmosphere at the club and I can assure you seeing bikers in action on the terraces with chains and the like was an unforgettable experience. They were generally known as the Tramps by us of a more 'smoother' persuasion, as it were, but certainly not to their face.

The violence that we thrived on back then was totally unorganised, it was spontaneous, just something that had to happen. You travel away, you went on the opposing ends, it was all about taking ends, everybody was fair game for it. From Plymouth (very tasty crew) to Newcastle, everybody was at it.

Another thing which began to develop more strongly was an unwritten code that those involved in hooliganism adhered to rigidly. There were things that simply were not done even back then, and the most important was that what happened at football stayed at football. At a time when most of the youth were still heavily influenced by the music of the era – and not just ska or rock and roll but also the growing soul scene – fighting in dance halls was a non-starter. If you ran into a rival group then it was best to simply avoid any kind of contact, otherwise you were out – and no one wanted that.

On match days, however, no such rules applied. And

as fighting in the streets around grounds increased across the country, the police finally began to tighten up. Following growing numbers of attacks on coaches carrying supporters and complaints from the hire companies, motorcycle escorts began to be given to fans coming by road. Yet incredibly, at some grounds, no such luxury was afforded to those who came by train. Often, fans would be let out at the same time after the match and the visitors simply left to run a gauntlet of abuse or worse as they made their way back to the station. When you remember that back then almost any rival fan was fair game, and that vandalism was rife, it must have been a horrific experience at some grounds.

In 1971, the hooligan problem was in the headlines again when Leeds fans rioted during a game against West Bromwich Albion. Needing a win to help their title challenge, the Leeds players were less than impressed when the referee gave a goal that is still argued over to this day. They surrounded and angrily jostled the referee but were then forced to protect him when between 30 and 40 supporters raced onto the pitch to join in the protest. The linesman was hit on the head with a rock and it took the police almost five minutes to restore order. Leeds lost the game and as a result, a little over two weeks later, Arsenal stole the title by a single point.

Following the game, Leeds officials came out and condemned the referee and linesman while almost condoning the actions of the fans. The FA were furious, hit the club with a £750 fine and ordered them to play the first four home games of the following season behind closed doors. It had been a deplorable episode and attracted even more negative coverage for the game.

By now, the police were really on the hooligans' case and a heavy uniformed presence could be expected at most games. For the fans, match days had settled into a fairly predictable pattern. Terrace battles and end-taking were still fairly frequent, as was trouble in the streets around grounds. However, another problem now began to surface: the throwing of missiles. Objects had always been thrown, of course, but things were becoming more sinister. Sharpened coins and darts were the favoured weapons, as they were easily concealed and could be thrown long distances with reasonable accuracy. Rarely were the police able to do anything about them. Even if they could have caught anyone – difficult enough given the sea of bodies to be found on most terraces – getting them out and arresting them without retaliation from their fellow fans was incredibly difficult. The only thing they could do was to search fans on the way in, and for the first time that began to happen at grounds on a wide-spread basis. Interestingly, many people involved in trouble saw the use of missiles as cowardly. Fighting was something you did with your fists and feet; hurling something indiscriminately was not what it was about.

It would be easy to believe that it was only the big clubs who were involved in trouble, but this was not the case. One club whose mob began to make a name for themselves was Norwich City. In February 1972, they played host to Millwall in front of 34,000 supporters and during incidents before and after the game, three people received stab wounds, one fan ended up in hospital with severe head injuries and 18 were arrested (interestingly, more locals than Londoners). From reports I have seen of this game, there were numerous confrontations between the two groups and it seems clear that the East Anglians were intent on using their infamous visitors to boost their own reputation. By all accounts, it worked. Later that same year, their home games with Liverpool, Spurs and

Arsenal, three of the 'worst' clubs around at that time, were marred by serious incidents.

Another mob known to cause trouble on their travels were Bristol Rovers. What follows is another extract from something sent to me by Chris B. It is part of an unpublished book about the 70s football and soul scene in Bristol and captures perfectly what it was like to be a part of football back then. At the request of the author I have taken out the names, but hopefully one day the book will make it into print.

We were playing City the following week at Ashton Gate. The Gloucester Cup was upon us, the annual finale to the season, a chance for the fans to prove themselves as the top dogs. It was always a murderous affair, no quarter asked, no quarter given. We had had an average season on the pitch but a spectacularly successful one off it; our rucks with QPR, Stoke, Leeds and Villa had hardened us up. We wanted the season to end on a high note and we were right up for it. We knew we had a boring three summer months in front of us and wanted to go out with a bang.

Word had gone out that we were meeting in The Star, opposite the ground, and everyone was going tooled up. The time had come to teach the East End scumbags a right lesson. Prove who was number one in the city.

I had left school with a clutch of 'O' levels and a metal hinge bracket from the side of a desk. About one foot long and solid steel, it made the perfect weapon. I stuffed it in the lining of my bomber jacket, praying to God I wouldn't be searched. The Monkey boots were brought out of the wardrobe and polished up – they were like old friends, I swear they smiled at me.

By the time I got to The Star, it was packed. Word had got round all right. Everyone was there and they were all tense. Nervous energy filled the air and ever-watchful eyes stared out of the windows. The City fans were gathering in their pubs and we were on their turf. We were expecting an attack and had placed a few younger spotters outside, dotted along Ashton Road. We were ready and waiting.

A breathless kid suddenly burst through the door: 'They're coming now, fucking hundreds of 'em!' We couldn't get out of the pub quick enough, picking up beer glasses and ashtrays on the way. The familiar guttural roar went up, the two tribes went to war, we clashed head on in the middle of the street, the same predictable violence. It was an ugly scene, one I was now accustomed to. It held no fears or terrors for me, it was all I wanted out of life; in my element. Pick a scumbag out of the melee, go for him, kick him, punch him, flailing arms like windmills. I felt utterly confident, the adrenaline was pumping, I had a superiority complex – no, it wasn't a complex, they *were* inferior. We were doing well, but by sheer numbers they were beginning to overwhelm us. The more you punched out, the more appeared, there seemed to be a limitless supply of the fuckers and, unbelievably, no coppers on the horizon. They outnumbered us, it was a familiar story. I looked around anxiously but I needn't have worried, everyone was staying firm. It was now the City fans' turn to suddenly look worried, they were looking past us. Beyond us out of our sight was an enormous horde of Rovers fans charging across

Ashton Park to back us up: 'We are the Tote End, we are the Tote End, we are the Tote End of EASTVILLE!' The reinforcements fired in, but the battle was all but over. City ran, we gave chase and whooped our delight; Rovers 1, City 0.

It didn't stop there, we made a beeline for the East End. All colours were hidden, the law were lining up to search us. I still had my bar hidden in my sleeve, I hadn't had a chance to use it in the street fight. Others hadn't been so reluctant to use theirs, there were some severe injuries. It was too late to ditch the weapon; I held my breath, my balls did their disappearing act again. The law were having an off-day – not only had they failed to break up the scrap in Ashton Road but they didn't seem interested in the hundred or so shifty-looking Tote Enders queuing up to get in the East End. We filed in quietly in ones and twos; we didn't want to be rumbled before we were all in.

Our main lad took the lead: 'Get in and move to the back, don't say a fucking word until we're all in place.' The East End was long and narrow, a gangway ran all the way at the back with just a small terrace, maybe nine feet wide, behind it. We positioned ourselves dead centre, right behind the main bulk of the East Enders. Once you had occupied this area it was very difficult for anybody to force you out. We all knew we could rely on each other, if you weren't up for it you wouldn't be there, it was as simple as that. We tried to blend in while everybody took up their positions, a few even chanted 'C-I-T-Y'. I couldn't though, it just stuck in my throat like a globule of phlegm. We waited, all eyes on our boy. We had no pre-arranged signal, we were just waiting for something to happen. The scumbags were going to get the shock of their lives. Unintentionally, the catalyst came from them: 'Rovers, where are you? Rovers, where are you?' they taunted the Rovers fans massed at the opposite end of the ground. Not for one minute did they think the enemy was in their camp, not two feet from their poxy noses. It was instantaneous: 'TOTE, TOTE, TOTE ENDERS! TOTE, TOTE, TOTE ENDERS!!' There was a millisecond of silence ... their jaws dropped quicker than a pair of whore's knickers. Tote Enders on their fucking manor and suddenly it was sheer bedlam as the City fans totally panicked. The ones nearest to us were trying to get away but they couldn't escape, it was like lambs to the slaughter. I could see the boot going in on some poor bastard lying on the ground, the worst place to be, and beyond that it was clear that weapons were being used. Bars and sticks, mostly; for all the bravado of carrying a knife, it was rare to see one being used back then.

Out of the corner of my eye I could see the law heading for us, truncheons drawn. All around was the aftermath of battle, bloodied bodies, scarves, shoes and youngsters crying. Did I feel sorry for them? Did I fuck. They should have gone in the enclosure with their old man, shouldn't they? Besides, he'll be doing the same to us in a few years time no doubt. The law had at last woken up, the dogs were barking and the truncheons were swinging. They were nicking anybody, some were still scrapping and kicking as they were grabbed round the neck and wrestled to the ground. 'You're fucking nicked, son!' – how many times had we heard that one? I was not to be spared, my arm was forced up my back: 'You, out! Come on, with me!'

'I ain't done fuck all!' I protested. I had been arrested before but only for vandalism and a bit of thieving as a kid. To be grabbed by a fat bastard of a copper who was determined to snap your arm off was another story.

'Honest, leave it out. Ow! You're breaking my fucking arm!' I shouted.

'I'll break your fucking neck in a minute, son!' he replied as he dragged me out, kicking and screaming.

I realised there were hundreds of pairs of eyes upon me, eyes full of hatred and venom . . . and fear. Yeah, that's right, I thought, we took your fucking end! I suddenly felt a lot better. They marched me into their brand new station which had been built inside Ashton Gate, all breeze block and corrugated iron. It was packed and chaotic, there was as many kiddies as coppers, all shouting and bawling, some snivelling and even some laughing. Fat copper sat me down and took my details. Well, details anyway, certainly not my real ones. I had a name, address and date of birth off pat. A new one for each season.

For some reason, the law were in a benevolent mood. Perhaps they were all Rovers fans but either way, I wasn't charged, just sat down and told to be quiet.

Once the game had finished and the crowd had gone, I was cautioned and sent on my way. I had got off lightly, unlike some of the poor bastards on the terraces. But that was football for us. And we'd certainly got our result.

Taking ends was still the favourite occupation of the hooligan gangs, but infiltrating the home territory was a dangerous business and not something to be done if you had no stomach for a fight. A trip to the toilet, for example, could often end in a battering if you had been identified but had not cottoned on to the fact. However, once a visiting group had managed to get some lads into the home end, it was only a matter of time before something happened. Either they were sussed and first abused and then attacked or, on a given signal, such as the teams running out or even the first goal, the interlopers would begin chanting and make themselves known. Whatever it was, once it started all hell broke loose. Taking someone's end was the ultimate humiliation for them and the ultimate result for you. For the supporters of some clubs, even getting onto an end and then giving it a bit of mouth as you stood next to a policeman was enough of a result, especially as in those days the police would often simply take you round the pitch and put you in with your mates rather than eject you. Occasionally, however, they would throw you out and leave you at the mercy of everyone waiting outside. And it was not unknown for the Old Bill at some grounds simply to leave you in the home end until you had received a few slaps from the local lads.

The clubs themselves had begun to realise that if they were ever to stop the haemorrhaging crowds, they would have to do something. In 1973 Nottingham Forest, having suffered both relegation and a fall in average attendance from over 20,000 in 1971–72 to under 10,000 in 1972–73, became one of the first clubs to erect pens to divide up the home terracing. Using 7ft-high steel fencing set in 4ft-square concrete foundations, the Trent End was split into four sections, each with a single and heavily policed entrance at the back. It proved an instant success. No longer were the crowds able to surge from side to side across the end, nor were those who caused trouble able to run off and lose themselves in the crowd. Now they were trapped, and the amount of trouble, at least on the Trent End, was reduced within weeks. The erection of those pens was significant in another respect: it showed that the game had just about given up trying to control the hooligans and had decided simply to cage them in instead. It was a decision that was to have massive and ultimately tragic implications.

That same year saw two other small but not insignificant developments. The first was that hooligan gangs started to leave their 'mark' wherever they went. Painted messages began to appear on walls near grounds, particularly in London, warning visitors that they were in someone else's territory. Similarly, some mobs even began to leave their 'badges' to show that they had been there despite the danger. The second thing of note was that for the first time, a gang of female hooligans came to national prominence.

It happened in Peterborough, when Derby County brought a massive mob to United for an FA Cup tie. After the game, 200–300 Derby fans went on the rampage as they made their way back to the station and a teenage girl on her way home from the match was confronted by a female Derby fan, who challenged her to a fight. When she refused, she was punched to the ground and then set upon by a group of girls wearing steel-capped boots. Eventually they were chased off but not before the victim had suffered a severe kicking and a suspected broken nose. The people who rescued her estimated that there were approximately a dozen of these females, none of them older than 15. Not one of them was ever caught.

The incident received widespread coverage in the papers but for once did not spawn copycat gangs. As a result, it remains one of only four incidents involving female hooligans I have ever heard about.

For as long as anyone could remember, fans, even hooligans, had been keen to let rival supporters know which team they followed. Scarves and hats were still the norm, as were badges. That had begun to change when the skinheads first arrived on the football scene. Their uniform of Ben Sherman, Levi Sta-Press, braces and Doc Martens quickly become synonymous with football violence, yet even they often carried scarves showing where their loyalties lay. Occasionally, some would even display scarves stolen from rival fans as battle honours. However, in 1973 some hooligans started to adopt odd quirks to their clothing. Gold or silver-painted Doc Martens, for example, were one way to show a bit of individuality, while others began wearing butchers' coats to games. Following the release of the controversial and extremely violent film *A Clockwork Orange* in 1971, some fans took individuality to the extreme, turning up at games wearing overalls, bowler hats and occasionally even make-up in deference to the 'hero' of the film. Thankfully, this practice didn't go on for long; it must have looked absolutely bizarre.

The following year, 1974, was to see yet another low point in the history of hooliganism; the first recorded football-related murder. On the second Saturday of the 1974–75 season, Bolton travelled to Blackpool for what was supposed to be a regular league fixture. Although the fans were searched for weapons going into the ground and kept apart on the terraces, under the stands, in the toilets and at the refreshment kiosks, rival supporters were able to mingle freely. At half-time it inevitably kicked off and during the fracas, someone produced an eight-inch sheath knife and a Blackpool fan was stabbed through the heart. The person who had lashed out with the knife was just 14 years old.

Although the murder sent shockwaves through the game, it can hardly have been a surprise. Stabbings had become commonplace and the sheer number of incidents of trouble in and around grounds was rising at an alarming rate. At the end of the previous season, about 400 Manchester United fans had invaded the pitch as relegation loomed and forced the game against Manchester City to be abandoned, while Newcastle were having to play all their home FA Cup ties behind closed doors because of trouble that had occurred during a quarter-final against Nottingham Forest the previous season. The game had simply had enough. It was time for action.

Following the example set by Everton and Nottingham Forest, clubs up and down the country began to erect perimeter fences to cage the fans in and keep them off the pitch. Together with the selective introduction of all-ticket games, it had a small but significant effect in calming down trouble inside grounds. For those games that were not all-ticket, the police adopted a more stringent policy of identifying the club loyalties of those entering grounds. The most important step, however, was that of segregation, not just inside grounds but outside as well. Escorts to and from stations and coach parks became the norm, and after games visiting fans would often be held until the home fans had dispersed.

For the hooligans, the challenge had been thrown down. Now, really for the first time, they began to change the way they conducted their affairs in direct response to what the authorities were doing. Inside the grounds, as movement became more difficult, groups began to abandon their traditional home end and instead moved to the stands adjacent to the visitors' enclosures. This allowed them to hurl both abuse and missiles at their rivals. It also allowed them to suss out who was who and, more importantly, afforded easier access directly outside the ground. Because of the restrictions afforded by the pens, taking ends began to die out as an activity, not only because it was difficult to get in but because it was difficult to get out should things go wrong. With entrance to the pens often quite restricted, if you sneaked in and kicked things off only to come unstuck, it could take an age for the police to get to you if you were at the front, especially if other supporters were making progress difficult for them.

The knock-on effect of the clampdown inside grounds was that outside, trouble increased. Organised specials were the usual form of transport for many fans but the police had begun to target them. To counter this, the hard-core hooligan groups began to abandon them in favour of 'unofficial' methods such as coaches – or, as they came to be known, thug buses – and pubs began to replace ends as the places to hit and protect. The added bonus this provided to the hooligans was that the trouble began to kick off earlier in the day, often long before opening time. Indeed, one of the favoured tactics among certain groups at the time was to turn up at the home mob's 'local' and force the landlord to open up and let you in early. By the time the regulars arrived you were already in residence, forcing them to either drive you out by force – which almost always led to the pub being wrecked and them being banned – or simply go to another pub and accept it as a defeat. There was always later on, after all. Often, however, rival fans would simply turn up en masse outside and invite a confrontation or, if they were one of the more powerful mobs, steam into the pub and wreck it. By the time the police turned up they would be long gone. Occasionally, just the act of walking past or even into the home fans' pub was a sign that the visitors were up for it. By 'sussing' or 'taking liberties', they were inviting a response. If none came, that in itself would be considered a result of sorts.

By the mid 70s, not only had the football authorities and the police finally started to take the hooligan problem seriously, the courts had begun to issue harsher sentences for any football-related offence. Despite this, the game experienced only a slight dip in the number of incidents. Indeed, for most people involved at that time, an appearance in court was deemed an occupational hazard. Wear a nice suit, look embarrassed and apologise was the usual tactic. Fight it and you fought the system – and usually lost. Fines were the norm, although the use of community schemes was on the increase. Many people actually preferred these because they were so poorly enforced that non-attendance often went unrecorded.

For the fans, things were changing fast. Not only had ska all but died off, but the skinhead culture looked like it was heading into history. The void was filled by soul, which exploded onto the scene. I have to say that I am, at heart, a soul boy. For me, the mid 70s to early 80s was *the* era. The bands, especially some of the British jazz-funk exponents, were brilliant and the concerts awesome. The only problem was the clothes, all flares and stupid haircuts. However, if the game thought the demise of the skinhead culture and the rise of Gary Glitter would have an effect on the hooligans, they were right. The problem was, rather than calming down, things got even worse.

The first signs of this came with the growing influence of the racist National Front at football. With black players beginning to make inroads into the game, the right wing saw football supporters as an obvious target for recruitment and soon publications such as *The Bulldog* were on open sale outside grounds. As increasing numbers of fans, both violent and non-violent, began to follow this doctrine, some of them began to adopt the skinhead style of dress but with clean-shaven heads. The image of skinhead was immediately and irreversibly damaged at that point and for the original skins, it must have been a sad end.

It is fair to say that most grounds had a right-wing element at this time but that was more a reflection of the age than anything else. Many mobs still had black members and it is reasonable to assume that many people who were involved with the NF at football back then did so more because of the fear and shock value it provided than for any political beliefs they held. It is also the case that many of those same people look back on that period with some degree of shame, and quite right, too.

By 1976, almost every club had fenced in its fans and the police had begun to try out an additional weapon, closed-circuit television (CCTV). Initially, the use of cameras and the dire warnings that accompanied it – if you're caught on film you will be arrested, if not today then maybe next week or next month – sent shockwaves through the hooligan world. Yet amazingly, legal concerns about their use caused a good deal of negative publicity and at some grounds they were withdrawn. But the hooligans had got the message. Trouble began to decrease inside grounds, but it exploded elsewhere.

For the London clubs, the underground had always been used to ambush rival fans, but now it took on added significance. Firms actually began to haunt specific stations in the hope of picking up stragglers. QPR, in particular, were well known for violence at Ladbroke Grove station, while Fulham Broadway was a non-starter if you weren't a Chelsea fan. On Saturday nights, Euston station would become like a battleground as fans of London clubs would scramble to get there before the northern clubs headed home or the Cockney Reds returned. Much the same could be said of all the mainline stations in the capital but trouble wasn't confined to London. Wherever fans had to change trains, problems were likely to kick off and attacks on trains, especially specials, became frequent. Wigan, especially, became known as 'ambush alley' as local fans threw missiles at every football train that passed.

Another regular venue for trouble was the motorway service stations. Indeed, some of the worst tales of violence from that period involve these oases of refreshment. Coachloads of fans from two, three and even four separate clubs would turn up and run riot before the police could get them loaded up and on their way, and for the station managers the arrival of these fans, escorted or not, meant only one thing: all their stock would vanish. Indeed, many fans made thieving a matter of principle on their travels as the belief that if you treat us badly, we'll act bad, was rife at that time. The inevitable result was that by about 1977, motorway service stations would only take football coaches if they pre-booked their arrival, so that the police could be present. And even then, they were accepted only reluctantly.

For the police, these were extra problems they did not need. They were also becoming increasingly aware that whatever they tried simply would not work. But the one thing they did have on their side was the law. This, coupled with the courts' growing exasperation with the hooligans' activities, meant that anyone who lodged a complaint against the police, legitimate or otherwise, had no chance of a sympathetic hearing. The fans began to realise that no matter what happened, the police would not be called to account.

In effect, the Old Bill now had free rein at football and they began to exploit it to the full. Any fan who travelled around from the mid 70s to the mid 80s will be aware that in many ways the police became the real enemy. Everyone suddenly became a potential hooligan and the abuse, intimidation and violence dealt out to fans in the name of law and order defied belief. For many, the worst were the Merseyside police; others name the Metropolitan force, others the Geordies. For me, later years were to show that certain members of the West Midlands constabulary were nothing less than animals. But the bottom line is that once the police began to adopt this approach, football fans in general began to feel persecuted, the hooligans' belief that the police were a natural enemy was reinforced, and the whole thing went into a downward spiral.

Before 1976 drew to a close, football suffered another serious blow with the death of a Millwall fan during a fight with West Ham supporters at New Cross station. So shocked were the authorities by this that the chairman of the Police Federation called on the government to suspend the game for a year to allow everything to calm down, a call that was totally ignored. Yet if this fatality was bad news for the game, within months it was to receive what was possibly the worst publicity it had ever had, in the shape of the now infamous *Panorama* documentary on Millwall supporters.

It is impossible to overstate the effect this programme had on football. Thanks to the tabloids, everyone in the country already knew about Millwall and their exploits, but now they could see them at first hand. Not only that, this firm had given itself both a name and a uniform. It was incredible stuff, seeing lads standing on terraces wearing surgical headgear and calling themselves The Treatment. They looked almost comical as they stood there with their colleagues, the Halfway Liners and F-Troop. But no one was laughing; it was too bloody frightening. It has been suggested on many occasions since that the lads who took part in this film made it all up for the cameras. I don't know if that is true or not. What I do know is that within days, almost every group in the land had given itself a name and Millwall had reached new heights of infamy.

Increasingly, calls were being made for the return of national service And although these usually came from backbench MPs desperate to make the papers, the idea was beginning to win support. In the end, however, there was a realisation that the youth would never accept such a move, and as all of them were potential voters – and many already were – the idea was shelved. These calls coincided with the rebirth of the skinhead movement and the emergence of the most anarchic scene the country had ever known, the punks.

If the original skins were hoping for a return to the old ways, then they were in for a rude awakening. The new-breed skins were even more overtly aggressive than their predecessors, and racism ran through the scene like a cancer. Many of this new breed openly enbraced fascist ideology and joined organisations such as the British Movement or the National Front. Together with the punks, they set out to forge an even wider division between young and old, with, it has to be said, huge success. In later years, bands such as Sham 69 and the Cockney Rejects latched onto their appeal among football fans and began to reflect it in their songs. Many even believe that the Sex Pistols classic, 'Anarchy In The UK', was written about hooliganism. In reality, punk had little influence on football, and after 1977, drugs began to make inroads into the scene and eventually it began to parody itself. However, the skins remained and the hooligan scene continued to grow.

The use of weapons during trouble was on the rise, especially knives. During Wolves' game with Manchester United at Molineux in 1978, for example, two men were stabbed, one in the back and one in a lung, while a hot-dog seller was tied to railings with some scarves and badly beaten. Horrific though it sounds now, such things were, sadly, fairly typical back then. Interestingly, not long after that, Wolves, who had always had a strong racist element among their crowd, began to experience an upsurge in Ku Klux Klan activity. The first evidence of this came when they played at Exeter in the FA Cup. At the initial game, which ended in a draw, Wolves fans had run riot in the city and caused massive amounts of damage to property. During the game, they had invaded the pitch four times and on one of those occasions had broken a crossbar. On the terraces, four men were seen wearing Klan headgear, something which drew wide coverage in the regional press. As the replay approached, local houses and pubs in the Midlands began to find KKK painted on walls and doorways while during the game, numerous Klan-style hoods were seen among the Wolves fans. At the time, the police claimed that these masks were being worn to prevent identification, as they were using CCTV at the game. But whatever it was about, it was a worrying development which, thankfully, died out as quickly as it had begun.

The same year, Millwall, who had yet again had their

ground closed after trouble against Ipswich, were forced to play their home matches in Portsmouth, a club with whom they already had a long-standing rivalry. As a consequence, every 'home' fixture saw serious trouble. At one game, against Bristol Rovers, the Millwall fans were involved in trouble with Rovers and Pompey fans, as well as with the newly formed Anti-Nazi League, who had taken exception to the Lions mob.

As the decade drew to a close, it was hard to believe that things could get any worse for football. Crowds were still dropping and the hooligan gangs, now sporting names and forming identities for themselves, were causing problems all over the country. As if that wasn't bad enough, they were also beginning to export hooliganism with them when English clubs played in Europe. Liverpool, Leeds and Manchester United fans had all caused trouble on their travels and at one point UEFA had expelled United from the Cup-Winners' Cup because of it, although they were reinstated on appeal.

Yet if the 70s had been bad, the 80s were to be even worse. And it all started with the birth of a movement that, unlike the Mods and the skins, did not adopt hooliganism but actually grew out from within it.

Chapter 4

The Dark Days

There should be no mistake here; from 1979 onwards, the Casuals *were* football violence. Indeed, it has always amazed me that a culture so prevalent and overtly violent should have received so little attention. One of the reasons for that seems to be that there are so many versions of what being a Casual was all about, and even how the whole thing started.

For me, being a Casual was about two things: football and clothes. Nothing else. On match days I would pull on my finest and head for Vicarage Road, or wherever, and the next day would revert to being R8123790 Corporal DA Brimson, the very picture of respectability. For others, an integral element of the Casual scene was music, primarily northern soul, Motown and/or jazz funk (and in later years electro, but we had best not mention that). Personally, as someone who, by the end of 1982, was not only a frequent face at all-nighters in the south east but was also DJing twice a week at a soul club near Oxford, I feel the two were entirely separate. I never knowingly linked the football and the music and, looking back, still

111

don't. However, the debate about the influence of the music scene on football is still raging almost two decades later although I have no intention of examining it here, as there are plenty of others who could do it far better justice than I.

The other debate surrounding the Casual scene concerns how it started, or to be more specific, who started it. The London clubs, particularly Chelsea, laid claim to this quite early on, asserting that they had begun to adopt a more 'discreet but stylish' form of clothing on the terraces to avoid the attentions of the police. There is some weight to this argument as I have seen pictures of supporters from London clubs in golf wear which were taken as early as 1979. Then again, I have also seen pictures of fans from the capital wearing 10-pin bowling shirts and brightly coloured cycling shirts. No, as a southerner it pains me to say it but the strongest claim, at least regarding the wearing of sports clothing, comes from the Scousers.

In the mid 70s, thanks to the Beatles, Jimmy Tarbuck and Cilla, the population of Liverpool had forged for itself a reputation for being quick-witted and friendly. However, any football fan of the same era will know that among the travelling fans of both Liverpool and Everton (and to a lesser extent Tranmere Rovers) were also some of the most violent and fearless fighters in the country. With a particular fondness for carrying, and using, Stanley knives, they were also renowned for indulging in widespread thieving on their travels. Indeed, when Everton came to Watford for the first time in 1983, almost every programme seller in the town was robbed. But as Liverpool travelled around Europe, their fans had taken to stealing expensive designer clothes on a grand scale, not just for themselves but to sell when they got back.

By the time 1980 was drawing to a close, people had begun to notice a new style on the terraces, one which was both smart and respectable. As this practice spread, fans around the country began to buy clothes from sports shops as well as golf and tennis clubs, and labels such as Fila, Pringle, Ellesse, Tacchini, Diadora and Lacoste began to appear. Ironically, this was totally against the whole concept of Casual. In an era when Margaret Thatcher was screaming her 'self-self-self' doctrine, wearing stolen clothes was, for many people, a kind of anti-rich statement. Buying clothes, or at least paying the full price, was simply falling in line with the current fashion and therefore consumerism. An interesting angle on this was sent to me some time ago. It comes from Pat, an exiled Chelsea fan from the Midlands.

> In about 1980–81, some pals and I went to see Chelsea play Liverpool at Anfield. The coppers escorted our coaches to a particular pub that had been allocated to us for the day. This pub must have been near the city centre because shortly after starting our first pint, a couple of Scouse kids came in. They were about 13 or 14 and one of them was holding some sheets of paper. These pieces of paper turned out to be photocopies of catalogues that had the details of various items of Casual clothing and footwear which they were prepared to rob to order, and sell on to us for exactly half the price advertised. I was able to kit myself out with a couple of Lyle & Scott jumpers and Nike trainers and was almost happy after losing to the Scousers yet again. And they wonder why we all think Scousers are robbing bastards?

On the terraces of the early 80s, style was everything. If

you went to football wearing the wrong label, or even the same clothes you had worn the week before, you became an object of ridicule. Clubs, and even regions, quickly developed set styles or adopted specific labels, and for those in the know it was even possible to work out which club a person followed by what he was wearing. Londoners, for example, always seemed to favour white trainers. The element of one-upmanship was vital to the scene. Styles seemed to change week in and week out, and a label that was essential one week would be old hat the next. Similarly, supporters coming into London, especially, would be vilified for their poor taste in clothes. And at a time when the north–south divide was huge in economic terms, much was made of the affluence afforded by living in the lower end of the country.

The media were slow to pick up on this style trend but among the first to realise what was happening was the then music journalist Garry Bushell. He labelled these fashion-conscious youths 'Herberts' but this term died out, to be replaced by the term Casuals. Following this, magazines such as *The Face* quickly picked up on it and although basically a music paper, it gave wide coverage to the fashion aspect. Letters talking about 'Terrace Chic' frequently appeared and often criticised rival club supporters for their poor dress sense.

The cost of some of this clothing was often phenomenal and it was not unusual to blow a week's wages on an outfit or even a single jacket. As a result, a new problem began to materialise, not for the police or even for the game but for the lads themselves. It was known to one and all as 'taxing' and it quickly became the bane of travelling football fans' lives. Quite simply, taxing involved having every item of clothing you were wearing stolen. If you were a fashion-conscious lad, this left you if not naked then pretty close to it. The fact that every penny you had would also be taken meant that getting home was also a major problem, something which led to much mirth on various trains and coaches and added to the humiliation.

For the police, the arrival of the Casuals proved a major headache. For now that the hooligans were no longer displaying colours, they had no obvious method of identifying what club they followed. The only way was to stop and question them, something that was not always possible when there were a large number of lads.

The arrival of the Casual scene and the style that accompanied it had not only altered the way the hooligans looked, but also the way that they thought of themselves. With their expensive clothes, they began to believe that they were a cut above the rest. As a result, they began to travel more independently of the 'scarfers' and the use of hired mini-buses and vans increased significantly. Indeed, often these vans, or as they later became known, battle buses, would travel in convoy and would carry formidable firms. For the police, this was a major problem as these buses could turn up anywhere and they had no obvious way of controlling them. In the early 80s, a few mobs adopted more outrageous forms of transport, many of which were designed with only one purpose in mind. I was told years ago that L*t*n fans would often travel to games in a large removal van and once they had found the home pub, would simply pull up outside, drop the tail gate and steam out. How true this is I do not know, but I have heard from a separate source that in about 1982 they staged a spectacular hit on the main Birmingham City pub using this method.

The van convoys were trouble enough when they

arrived in towns for games, but they also began to cause problems when they stopped en route. As my home town is about an hour from London, it became a favourite stop-off point for mobs heading out of the capital on a Saturday night. Everton in particular would stop in a certain pub whenever they were down south and this inevitably resulted in trouble from the locals, many of whom would be arriving home from Chelsea, Spurs or Arsenal at around the same time.

However, not everyone had the option of going by road and the specials were still widely in use. But by now, the wrecking of carriages had become commonplace and it was not unusual for trains to be held until the transport police turned up to arrest anyone caught damaging rolling stock. Indeed, it was rare for a light bulb still to be working when a special arrived home. In 1980, British Rail banned alcohol on these trains. Then, as more and more fans began to try to evade the police by using scheduled services, this bylaw was extended to include any train on which it was believed football fans would be travelling.

On the terraces, things were getting significantly worse as football entered what was to become its darkest age. On 6 September 1980, a 17-year-old Middlesbrough fan was stabbed to death outside Ayresome Park during a disturbance involving Nottingham Forest supporters. That same day Sheffield Wednesday fans forced a 29-minute stoppage at Oldham, during which time their manager Jack Charlton was hit on the head with a missile as he pleaded with the crowd to behave. Fans hurled bricks and coins at each other before scaling the fences and fighting on the pitch. In the course of the brawling, 20 people were hurt including a number of policemen. But at that point in time, West Ham were the club to watch and certainly to be wary of. Earlier that year they had caused serious trouble in Newcastle at a game best remembered for the first recorded use of a petrol bomb inside a ground. Ironically, it was thrown *into* the West Ham enclosure by Newcastle fans. On the same day as the murder of the Boro fan and the trouble involving Sheffield Wednesday, West Ham went to Stamford Bridge and during mayhem in and around the ground, 42 people were arrested.

By this time, the hooligans had started to become more organised. In the 70s, what planning there had been had largely revolved around travel and drinking, and although there were exceptions fights had, generally speaking, been spontaneous affairs. But as the Casual scene became more entrenched, firms began to plan in advance. If phone numbers of rival groups were known, contact would be made and challenges issued (in later years, the personal columns in magazines such as *Sounds* would be used to place adverts announcing where they would be and at what time on specific match days). Another development was the increasing use of spotters, young lads who went out looking for rival firms or mobs and then reported their whereabouts back to the main group. It was widely believed that in London, West Ham had a group of lads on mopeds to ferry information around.

Hooligan tactics varied from club to club. Both Manchester United and Chelsea had so many lads willing to be involved that they would simply flood areas and grounds and invite trouble. Another Chelsea tactic would be to leave town after a game and then return two or three hours later and hit the home fans in a pub or club. West Ham, on the other hand, still favoured infiltration into grounds and had enough lads who had the bottle, or stupidity, to try it on everywhere they went. Millwall simply spread fear before them.

Weapons were also coming into frequent use and in this area, too, the hooligans were developing variations of their own. Millwall, inevitably, had taken the lead with what was known as the 'Millwall Brick'. Quite simply, it was made from a newspaper which, when folded in a particular way, soaked in water and left to dry in the sun, became as hard as iron. When held in the fist, it was as good as any knuckleduster ever was. The 'beauty' of the Millwall Brick was that it could be constructed quite easily once inside the ground, thus avoiding problems if you were searched.

Another weapon which came into use around this time was the dual-cut Stanley blade. This was two blades taped together with a matchstick in between them. The resultant cuts, being so close together, were all but impossible to stitch properly, which meant that the scars were huge. Somewhat bizarrely, one of the favourite places for slashing someone was across the backside because it meant that the victim could not sit down for weeks, until the scars had healed. Other weapons which emerged were gold balls with small slivers of Stanley knife blade stuck to them with superglue, cigarette packets full of rocks, and small 'puff'-type bottles full of ammonia, which were sprayed into people's faces. Some firms even used to carry pockets full of marbles or ballbearings with them. When things kicked off and the mounted police turned up, these would be rolled along the road in front of the horses.

For the authorities, the big worry about the Casuals was that they were becoming almost cult heroes at some clubs. As a result, they were attracting new followers and so the numbers involved in hooliganism were increasing. Clubs had CCTV inside grounds, but many were complaining that the costs involved did not warrant it. West Ham were one club who began using it early on but, strangely, would often only eject those who were causing problems rather than detain them.

In 1982, things hit a new low with yet another football-related death. A supporter had already died from asphyxia during trouble between Manchester United and Spurs fans on the underground at Seven Sisters the previous November, but when an Arsenal fan was stabbed to death in May after the game with West Ham, pinned to his chest was a calling card on which were the words: 'Congratulations, you've just met the ICF.' Inevitably, the press went mental and, just as predictably, within days firms up and down the country were producing their own.

Inside the ground that day, West Ham had staged a massive and spectacular hit on their North London rivals. Having infiltrated the North Bank, they let off a smoke bomb and, at a time when the IRA were waging a bombing campaign in England, it caused severe panic. But for the West Ham lads, all of whom knew what was happening, the smoke was the signal to kick things off and they surged across the terrace. Before the Arsenal firm could regroup, the police had surrounded the West Ham supporters and it was all over. The ICF had taken the Arsenal home end; it was another major victory.

At Chelsea, following severe crowd trouble at Derby earlier in the season, the club had been told by the FA that all their away games would be made all-ticket until the turn of the year. Although this was later reversed on appeal, the club finally decided, after trouble at their FA Cup fifth round tie at home to Liverpool, that the time had come to go on the offensive. The front cover of the programme for the quarter-final against Spurs in March carried a direct threat against the hooligans, stating that any caught causing trouble inside the ground would be banned for life and also prosecuted by the club. It was to have little or no effect and one of the main reasons for that was because, increasingly, other clubs were bringing trouble of their own when visiting the Bridge. This rarely caused the Chelsea firm any problems, as the Blues still had one of the fiercest mobs in the country. But one of the few mobs able and willing to take them on, were Leeds United.

In October 1982, following Leeds' relegation to the Second Division, where Chelsea had by now taken up residence, the Elland Road faithful came to London ready to kick it off with their old adversaries. What they did not expect was for Chelsea to ambush them at Piccadilly Circus. However, for the London mob things did not go according to plan and the Leeds fans stood and fought before the police turned up. According to people I have spoken to from both clubs, as soon as the Old Bill arrived, Chelsea scattered into the side streets and although some Leeds fans went after them, the bulk turned their fury on the police and attacked them with metal bars, wooden planks and scaffold poles stolen from a building site nearby. In all, 153 supporters were arrested at this incident, almost all of them from Yorkshire. But this was only one of at least three or four mobs Leeds had in the capital that day and at the game itself, another 60 were arrested following even more trouble. Again, almost all were Leeds fans. However you look at it, this was, for the Yorkshire club, a massive invasion.

For the return fixture the following February, Chelsea prepared to go to Elland Road seriously mobbed up. But as a train full of Chelsea supporters pulled in to Wakefield station, four petrol bombs were thrown from an adjacent

Royal Mail sorting office car park which had an open and unobstructed view of the platform. The first hit the roof of the first carriage, the second overshot and hit a police dog, the third landed on the tracks and the fourth scored a direct hit on one of the windows. Thankfully, the train was an Inter City 125 and the windows were double-glazed; if it had been an older-style train and the window had smashed, who knows what could have happened? For those on the train, this was a terrifying experience and when it finally arrived in Leeds, a few refused to get off. Word of the attack spread among the Chelsea fans at a rapid rate and this, coupled with a very strong and oppressive police presence, ensured that little happened that day. But for Leeds, it was, again, another victory.

Later that year, in October, the two clubs were involved in yet another tragedy. When Huddersfield played host to Chelsea, approximately 100 Leeds fans turned up and began a series of running battles with the home fans. After the game, all three sets of supporters were involved in numerous incidents and a Chelsea supporter was badly beaten with pool cues. Sadly, he was to die from his injuries that night.

In November 1983, the image of the English game suffered a further knock when Spurs fans rioted in Rotterdam after their victory over Feyenoord and England fans again laid waste to Luxembourg. By now UEFA were seriously concerned about what was happening and warned the FA that unless they sorted things out, English clubs would be banned from Europe, a warning that was to come to fruition sooner rather than later. Not only were the FA now under the eagle eye of UEFA, they had also come under the increasing scrutiny of the government, who had begun to take an interest in the problem. However, on the plus side, the police were finally turning to more advanced methods of security at games and were increasingly using CCTV and hand-held cameras to record trouble and identify known hooligans. In 1984, they obtained their first convictions using film of trouble. Four supporters were sent down after footage of an off involving Huddersfield and Leeds supporters was shown in court.

The Casual scene was now at its height. Trouble was almost inevitable at most games and yet still things happened which stunned those who were either involved or simply observers. As firms sought to enhance reputations, hits and ambushes became even more daring and more organised, and possibly the most famous of these involved Bristol City and Millwall. This incident was covered in depth in the book *Capital Punishment*, but in a nutshell: Millwall had travelled to Bristol and caused mayhem. Locals had been stabbed and another had ended up with a broken back. Eventually, the City mob had got themselves organised and two Millwall fans were thrown off a bridge. A few weeks later, Bristol City had travelled to London for another game and had staged a totally unexpected attack on Millwall's main pub. With these scores to settle, Millwall fans now planned a hit on a scale that was, up to that point, unprecedented. When City came to Millwall later that season, the supporters' coaches were directed down a dead end, miles away from The Den, where a massive Millwall mob were waiting. The planning and precision of this hit was almost military-like and it worked perfectly. More importantly, the reputation of the Millwall fans as fearless was at a new height – only to be exceeded just a few months later in March when they travelled to L*t*n and rioted in full view of the television cameras.

If the 80s had been bad up to that point, 1985 was, and

remains, the worst year for football violence. Indeed, the Kenilworth Road disorder remains possibly the most highly publicised incident of hooliganism ever seen. Inevitably, England's campaign to stage Euro '88 was finished as soon as the first seat was ripped up and thrown, but more worryingly for the game, the government was furious. FA chiefs were summoned to Downing Street for a severe bollocking but unfortunately, Ted Croker, then secretary of the FA, told Margaret Thatcher that hooliganism wasn't a football problem at all, it was society's. Therefore, it was nothing to do with the game and any resolution could only come via the government. One can only guess at her reaction to this, but immediately the government drew up plans for a national ID card system for football fans and, for good measure, banned the sale of alcohol at matches.

The chairman of Chelsea, Ken Bates, also decided that he had had enough of the hooligans among his support and decided to take action on his own. First, in protest at the continued reporting of trouble at Stamford Bridge, he banned a section of the press who he felt were wholly to blame for giving the club a negative image. More controversially, in an effort to prevent pitch invasions, he erected an electric fence in front of the home supporters. His right to do this was challenged in court by the Greater London Council and it was never switched on. And if Bates had simply intended to send a message to fans everywhere, it went unheeded.

On 11 May 1985, the same day that 56 people died in the Bradford fire, Leeds fans ran riot at Birmingham City's ground, resulting in injuries to 96 policemen and the death of a young boy when a wall collapsed. Football went into shock. Yet worse was to come when just 18 days later, Liverpool fans caused the death of 39 Italian football fans when they charged across a terrace at the Heysel Stadium in Brussels before the European Cup final. Much was made at the time of the failure of the Belgian police operation at the match, but the bottom line is that the Liverpool fans and the culture of violence inherent in the English game at that time were totally to blame. Within days, UEFA had banned English clubs from European competition indefinitely, with Liverpool having a further three-year ban on top of that. Manchester United, Norwich, Everton and Southampton, four of the five clubs who had qualified for Europe that season, challenged this ban in the High Court, claiming it was unfair because it had nothing to do with them. Thankfully, the courts upheld the decision and the clubs were out. Yet before the dust had settled, the game suffered a further kick in the teeth when the ICF were featured in another television documentary.

The Inter City Firm, so called because of their favoured method of travel, had long been one of the most notorious of the football mobs. Their reputation for fearless fighting and meticulous planning was well deserved and they were held in awe by many fans the length and breadth of the country. I saw them in action at close quarters only once and that was enough. Nutters is a word that springs immediately to mind. The notoriety of the ICF was further enhanced by the numerous myths and legends that surrounded them at the time. It was widely believed, for example, that the firm consisted largely of City traders who, thanks to their huge salaries, funded everybody else's travel. Another rumour circulated was that the group planned to copyright the ICF logo and market a range of Casual clothing under it. How true any of this was is a matter of debate, but one thing is sure: the programme took their infamy to new heights.

Furthermore, it had the knock-on effect of firing up the hooligan firms again as they began to distance themselves from the tragedy of Heysel. The feeling at the time was that this was very much a Scouser problem.

The documentary reawakened media interest in the whole issue of organised football violence and individual firms and, as usual, copycat gangs began to appear all over the place, each claiming that they had done this or that and were 'top dogs' in the hooligan world. Unknown to the hooligans, however, changes were afoot. While they carried on causing havoc around the country, the police had finally resolved to smash the organised groups once and for all. They had decided to go undercover.

The Metropolitan Police were the first to show their hand with 'Operation Own Goal' (a title that was to prove unintentionally prophetic) which targeted the Chelsea firm among others in 1985–86. When arrests were made and the police operation was revealed, the impact on hooligans throughout the country was major. After all, if Chelsea could get infiltrated and then turned over by the Old Bill, what chance would most of the others have? The government had also gone on the offensive with legislation in the shape of the Sporting Offences Act and a revised Public Order Act. These, together with the increasing use of CCTV, proved once and for all that hooliganism was being taken seriously. Almost immediately, there was a sharp decline in trouble at games and although it didn't solve the problem completely, for the first time things were looking up – at least for football. The 1985–86 season was to mark the low point in attendances, after which there has been steady increases.

Yet still things took place which left people on the outside shaking their heads in disbelief. At the end of the 1985–86 season, UEFA had relaxed the ban on English clubs to allow them at least to play friendlies overseas. Unfortunately, two of the first clubs to take advantage of this were West Ham and Manchester United, and when a boat set out from Harwich for the continent, with what the ferry company believed to be 130 Manchester United fans on board, the truth was that 30 of them were from the East End. With an eight-and-a-half-hour trip ahead of them, trouble soon broke out in the bars and, with no police on board, it quickly escalated. With no sign of things calming down, the captain was forced to turn the ship round and head back to Harwich. When it docked in England and the police boarded, 14 people were arrested, four were taken to hospital with serious stab wounds and another 30 had injuries caused by flying glass. Neither UEFA nor the FA was impressed.

By this time L*t*n T*wn had begun the ultimately doomed experiment of banning away fans and the police were clamping down all over. Some of those who had been serious players in the hooligan game now began to become concerned about preserving their liberty and started to drift away from the scene. Those who remained, however, kept themselves in tight groups and became even more organised.

Outside of football, the organised side of hooliganism was still something of a mystery. Some light was shed on it in 1987, however, with the release of the film *The Firm*. With a brilliant cast led by Gary Oldman, the story was very much a product of its time but it remains possibly the best football-related film to date. The brutality of hooliganism was laid bare for all to see, as was the sheer folly of it all. Yet if anyone was hoping it would make the hooligans stop and think about what they were doing, they were, of course, mistaken. If anything, some of the smaller, less organised groups treated *The Firm* like a guide showing them how it should be done. The use of knives increased again, as did the sheer ferocity of some of the violence.

In the 1987–88 season, however, the actual number of reported incidents continued to decline and it was not until the end of the season that anything serious enough happened to warrant major media attention. At a time when play-offs were used to decide who remained in the First Division, a meeting over two legs between Chelsea and Middlesbrough was always going to be volatile, and so it proved. At Stamford Bridge, with Chelsea losing 2–0 on aggregate from the first leg, the fans tried to force the abandonment of the game without success. This led to serious crowd disorder both inside and outside the ground, and 102 arrests were made. With Euro '88 only a matter of weeks away, England and its fans were placed firmly in the spotlight and the FA hit Chelsea with an immediate £75,000 fine, fearing that England might be thrown out of the championships. Thankfully, that did not happen but there was more trouble involving England fans at the tournament in Germany (albeit not as much as the media would have had the country believe) and it was beginning to look as though all the good work accomplished since Heysel was being undone.

In fact, hooliganism continued to decline and a major reason for this was that a new culture was emerging among the youth: the rave scene. The attractiveness of the dance scene to young males at that time cannot be underestimated. For not only did it involve the obvious combination of music, dance and women, it also included a subversive element. Illegal raves in warehouses and fields often involved chasing around the country trying to evade the police, and this was incredibly exciting for those who were a part of it. The explosion of drugs that surrounded this scene also had a major impact on hooliganism, because if you were doped up to the eyeballs, the last thing you wanted to do was fight anyone.

The police attitude to football fans, however, remained unchanged. All were potential hooligans and all were to be treated as a possible threat. And then came the event that changed everything: Hillsborough.

The events in Sheffield on that fateful day, 15 April 1989, have received massive exposure over the years and quite rightly so. Much has been made of the police actions, while a lot less has been made of the simple truth that if Liverpool supporters without tickets had not been trying to force their way in – as they and others had done a thousand times before – those 96 souls would still be alive today. But the stark reality is that those people died as a direct result of the threat of hooliganism. Arguments about which end the Liverpool fans should have been in and why a cordon wasn't in place at the end of Leppings Lane are largely irrelevant. If people had not caused trouble in the past, there would have been no need for fences and we would not have arrived at the point where all football fans were demonised. So rather than believe that the crowd were fighting in those pens or trying to invade the pitch, the police would have immediately realised that they were being crushed to death. We are all to blame in part for what happened at Hillsborough because, as fans, we either played our part in dragging the game down to that point or we simply sat back and watched while others did it.

The subsequent Taylor Report finally forced the game to get its act together and sort itself out. The fences came down and all-seater stadia became compulsory in the top flight. Furthermore, the ID card scheme, which the government was still advocating, was finally abandoned. Most important, however, was the sudden realisation among the general public and the police that football fans were not all hooligans; most were actually human. As a result, attitudes changed and, finally, the police began to take a more sympathetic approach in their role at football.

The following season was one of the quietest for many a year and the country began to believe that, finally, things had changed. But all that work was undone in a few short hours when on the final day of the season, Leeds travelled to Bournemouth needing a win to secure both promotion and the Second Division title. The police, anticipating disorder at this game as soon as the fixture list had been announced the year before, had been calling for months for the game to be moved from the Bank Holiday weekend to earlier in the season. But the Football League had ignored their pleas and insisted the game go ahead as scheduled. As a result, over 5,000 Leeds fans travelled and down on the seafront many of them ran amok; 104 arrests were made over the weekend and at one point, police in riot gear had to quell a major off on the beach. The Football League were shamed into handing the police a veto for all future games which might produce problems.

A few weeks later, England travelled to the Italia '90 World Cup, where more problems broke out among the fans. Yet this time England fans were largely seen as the victims and as the 1990–91 season started, there was a new feeling about the game. The mood was more positive and as the rave scene continued to draw people away from the hooligan scene, it was widely felt that football was witnessing the dying embers of the problem. It was to be a false dawn.

Early that season, the ICF came to the attention of the

media yet again. For some time, a well-known brand of washing powder had been running a promotion offering cheap rail tickets to its customers, something many football fans, not just the West Ham supporters, had exploited to the full. However, the slogan they had used was 'Surprise a friend this weekend' and when a Millwall fan was found stabbed following a confrontation, on his chest was pinned the front of one of these packs. On the back of it, someone had written: 'Nothing personal, the ICF.'

By this time, thanks to problems with the police evidence, Operation Own Goal had collapsed in a blaze of publicity and the majority of the convictions obtained had been quashed on appeal. Furthermore, other police operations against hooligan groups had also failed and the whole concept of undercover work was being called into question. Yet the very idea of it continued to concern those still actively involved in violence and many began to scale down their involvement. Others were smarting from the fact that the police finally seemed to have got the upper hand in the battle. They were now using video cameras as a matter of routine and CCTV was spreading through grounds, and even outside, at an alarming rate. Some of the groups began to look at ways to fight back; others simply looked for new ways to inflict damage.

In late 1990, certain individuals cottoned on to the fact that the best way to avoid the police was to find out where they were and what they were doing. This led to the growing use of radio scanners so the firms could listen in to police frequencies. That same year saw one of the early uses of a weapon that was to become a regular tool of the hooligan groups, CS gas. Almost inevitably, it involved West Ham but this time they were the victims as Leicester City supporters used the gas on them as they waited outside Filbert Street.

As the implementation of the Taylor Report continued, trouble inside grounds, at least in the top flight, was becoming less and less frequent. So much so that there were even suggestions that, finally, the problem had been solved altogether, an idea the game and the police were happy to encourage. But in the lower divisions, little was changing. Terracing was still in place and many of the lads who had deserted or been banned from the big clubs after Hillsborough made their way down the divisions or even into the non-league scene. Indeed, for many, life outside the professional game was just like the good old days and the grass-roots game began to experience a small but significant rise in incidents at matches.

If football genuinely thought that hooliganism was a thing of the past, it was only deluding itself. In February 1992, the first serious pitch invasion inside an English ground for two years forced the issue back onto the front pages of the papers. At St Andrews, Birmingham City fans invaded the pitch and one of them attacked the referee after Stoke City had scored a late equaliser. The referee was forced to take the players off the pitch and, after the ground was cleared, they were brought back on to play out the last 35 seconds in an almost empty stadium. The FA went mad and after the Birmingham chairman had all but blamed the invasion on the ineptitude of the match officials, he was hit with a misconduct charge and the club handed a £50,000 fine and told to play two matches behind closed doors. It was a sad incident, but it marked a significant change. Violence inside grounds began to increase again and later that same year, the Kingstonian goalkeeper was hit on the head by a coin thrown from among the Peterborough United supporters during an FA cup tie. There was more missile-throwing later that year, this time during a Coca-Cola Cup tie. At Arsenal, Ian Wright was hit on the head by a coin thrown from an enclosure holding Millwall supporters and in the return leg, Nigel Winterburn was struck by another object.

As the game moved into 1993, the hooligans were becoming braver again as the threat of CCTV had proved to be less dangerous than they had first suspected. There was a growing realisation that if you were not arrested on the day, it was unlikely you would be arrested at all.

At the last ever game at The Den, Millwall supporters almost ripped the place to shreds just weeks before the bulldozers moved in to demolish it. Within the first few weeks at their new all-seater home, ironically a stadium designed to discourage hooliganism, serious trouble broke out again and the Charlton chairman was attacked. As if this wasn't bad enough, come the end of the season things would sink to a new low at the club. Having made the play-offs, Millwall played host to Derby County but during the game, horrific racial abuse was directed at the two black players in the Derby side. So intimidating was the atmosphere that they were both substituted before the end of the game. When the final whistle blew, the Millwall fans invaded the pitch and the Derby keeper was attacked. Yet what happened inside the ground was only half the story. Before the game, the two sets of fans had staged a massive fight at Rotherhithe. The police had managed to calm the situation but after the game, all hell broke loose. As well as serious disorder outside the New Den, fighting also carried on down on the underground as the Derby fans battled their way back to their trains. These incidents saw possibly the first use of something that was to become an essential tool in later years, the mobile phone. As the trouble unfolded, fans on both sides were seen to use them to call up reinforcements. Subsequently, as mobiles became more widely available, not to mention smaller, their use at matches increased markedly.

With this new tool at their disposal, the mobs became seriously organised and the pre-arranging of offs became the norm as rival gangs could locate each other almost instantly. The key to this, of course, was getting hold of the other person's number, but that was a lot easier than it might sound. The usual way was to obtain it off someone else via the hooligan grapevine. Similarly, many numbers were exchanged with other hooligans on trips abroad with England or even in the pubs around Wembley. Another way was simply to shout them at each other inside grounds (something I witnessed on a number of occasions at Vicarage Road) and it was even known for stewards to innocently pass numbers across terracing at one time. Thankfully, this practice was stopped when clubs began to wake up to what was happening. Despite this alarming development, the general feeling was that trouble was still not a serious problem. More and more 'respectable' fans were going to games in perfect safety. Often they would go for weeks, if not months, without seeing a hint of trouble.

A warning of problems to come arrived from an unlikely source when in 1994 a video entitled *Trouble on the Terraces* was released. Narrated by the actor Sean Bean and featuring a host of academics, it was supposed to be a serious examination of the hooligan issue. What it actually was was a cynical attempt to exploit a gap in the market and it worked perfectly. With footage of fights and pitch invasions, its market was obvious and it sold by the bucketload. The police were far from happy and neither were the FA.

Then on 25 January 1995, during a match at Selhurst Park, Eric Cantona, of Manchester United and quite possibly their greatest ever player, was sent off against Crystal Palace. As he walked along the touchline to the dressing-rooms a Palace fan ran down to the front of the stand and began gesturing and hurling abuse at the Frenchman who, within seconds, had lunged at him with a kung-fu style kick. When this failed to connect, Cantona jumped up and lashed out with his fists before his team-mates and various stewards managed to drag him away. The pictures were beamed around the world and to head off any criticism, United banned Cantona for the rest of the season. The spotlight was then turned on the fan concerned and he was blamed for inciting the reaction. From this, the focus switched to the behaviour of fans in general and suddenly the media were showing renewed interest in the activities of the organised firms. Right on cue, at an FA Cup tie Chelsea and Millwall fans were involved in some of the most serious hooliganism ever seen in the capital. It took over 200 officers and 12 police horses to keep the fans apart at the New Den but as the game ended in a draw, the police were faced with the unenviable task of dealing with the replay, where the violence at Stamford Bridge was of a level unprecedented in recent times. Inside the ground, two Millwall players were attacked by Chelsea fans as they left the field, and outside, the supporters from the East London club turned their attention to the police, attacking them with CS gas and leaving 20 officers injured. In all, 38 arrests were made.

Coverage of the trouble at the two games was huge and there was a feeling among the hooligan groups that the 'good old days' were returning. For football, these were worrying times. But if the authorities thought the worst had passed, they were mistaken. Dublin was but days away.

As with many aspects of the hooliganism debate, what happened in Dublin has been covered in depth in one of my previous books, *England, My England*, and there seems little point going over it again. However, as a result of what happened at that game, the media spotlight was turned on the background of the hooligans involved, especially those arrested. Life stories, families and careers were dissected and explored in minute detail. Yet again, the fact that some were in very well-paid jobs astonished journalists who still genuinely believed they must all be braindead thugs who craved publicity. For the fans, the other concern was that the extreme right wing had emerged again, and very few wanted to be tarred with that particular brush. Indeed, shortly after Dublin, the extreme left seemed to take a renewed interest in football, targeting clubs with right-wing followings and partaking in some serious acts of violence against them.

Before the dust could settle, more trouble involving English fans erupted. When Chelsea travelled to Belgium just two weeks after Dublin, the police were forced to use water cannon on ticketless fans and then arrested 354 of them before deporting almost a thousand more. In the next round, the Chelsea faithful travelled to Zaragoza in Spain and were, quite simply, battered senseless by the local police. Events at these two games, however, should not be thought of as 'English hooliganism'. The trip to Belgium was notable for the fact that the locals mobbed up and took the fight to Chelsea, while at the game in Spain the Chelsea fans came under indiscriminate and violent attack from the police. Despite the obvious anger shown by those returning to England, neither the football authorities nor the government took action on the fans' behalf – something which sent a clear message both to the fans and the hooligans themselves.

Just a few weeks later, the game was to witness yet another tragedy. Before the FA Cup semi-final replay at Villa Park between Crystal Palace and Manchester United, a Palace fan was crushed to death under the wheels of a coach as he attempted to escape from United fans who had kicked trouble off outside a Midlands pub. The incident attracted even more unfavourable publicity for football at a time when it could ill afford it. For lurking on the horizon was Euro 96, the largest tournament England had staged since the World Cup in 1966.

Already, following Dublin, there had been calls for the country to give up the tournament. After the problems involving Chelsea fans, these became even louder. Such calls were ignored, but the trouble at the end of the 1994–95 season had set a pattern. The media went into overdrive, warning about the potential for trouble the following summer involving English lads and also those from abroad who were looking to settle scores with the England fans. For their part the police, desperate to foster the belief that they had the hooligans under control, issued press release after press release talking about arrest figures and intelligence reports and warning the hooligans that if they stepped out of line, they would be hammered. For the firms, this was just the kind of challenge they relished. All the talk was of the so-called England 'superfirm', involving the top boys from all the clubs in England. There were even suggestions that all the firms would link up and fight alongside each other. It was all totally ridiculous, of course, but it made for some entertaining press.

In the event, Euro 96 – which is also given extensive coverage in *England, My England* – passed off fairly peacefully, the Scotland and Germany games against England apart. But the media had hyped up the hooligan gangs so much that trouble the next season was inevitable.

The tournament had also equipped the country with a new love of the game. Many had even discovered it for the first time. For the fighting firms, this caused a major rethink. By now, it was accepted practice that scarfers, as they had become universally known, were not fair game and anyone dishing out any kind of violence to them was open to ridicule from their peers. And in a culture where reputation is everything, such things are almost sacred. As a result, it became normal practice at some clubs to locate visiting mobs when they came to town and then for one member of the home firm to visit them personally and suss out if they wanted to kick things off or not. If they didn't, for whatever reason, then they were simply left alone; if they were game, phone numbers were exchanged or they were invited to a specific location at a specific time. This method avoided both the attentions of the police and the involvement of innocent fans. The latter were rarely, if ever, attacked. They were almost regarded as being neutral and therefore untouchable.

But if Euro 96 had encouraged a new breed of fan, it also attracted some old blood. Suddenly, familiar faces began emerging on the stands and terraces around the country, returning to the game after years away dancing and popping pills. They were looking to recapture both their youth and the buzz they received from being involved in trouble, and their reappearance was a major concern both to rival firms and to the police. For the hooligans, the worry was that some of these older lads were fearless and would not run. But they also knew what was what as regards the law. Now in their late thirties and early forties, they simply would not allow themselves to be treated disrespectfully by the police, who became wary of both the internal disciplinary and legal repercussions of their own actions.

The firms were also beginning to devise even more ways to combat police interference in their activities. It was becoming increasingly common for them to send scouts into away grounds to suss out which areas were not covered by CCTV and if they found one suitable, then that was where they stood and, if possible, fought. Pagers also began to come into vogue as the police were becoming suspicious of people using mobiles inside grounds. But most worrying of all was the fact that the Casual scene was making a major comeback. Suddenly new labels began appearing and although the scene had never really died off, these signalled a return to the original concept. Flash and arrogant, a dangerous combination. Once again, trouble began to increase although interestingly, according to the police figures, it was still on the decline – something which I suspect had rather more to do with their containment tactics than reality.

Proof of this seemed to come at the beginning of 1998 when the game in England experienced a huge upsurge in hooligan activity. It was the nature of some of these incidents that was most alarming, especially the attacks on officials which seemed to be a regular feature during the first few months of the year. The first came at Portsmouth when a Sheffield United fan jumped onto the pitch at Fratton Park and knocked out a linesman. In April, a supporter ran onto the pitch at Everton but was detained before he could get at the ref. The same day, Liverpool players had to wrestle fans to the ground to prevent an attack on the referee at Barnsley. And still on the same day, a Fulham fan was killed during disturbances at Gillingham.

In the build-up to the World Cup, which was just weeks away, this was the worst possible news for the game. Already fears had been expressed about the possibility of trouble at the tournament involving England fans, and the police had been hard at work sorting out potential troublemakers. Indeed, just a week before the tragic death of Matthew Fox, the Fulham supporter, 19 known English hooligans were prevented from entering Switzerland where England were playing a friendly. The day after that, police raided the houses of 29 men in Sunderland in an effort to prevent trouble in France that coming summer. Inevitably, the media got in on the act. More speculative and provocative headlines spewed out and the government began warning of dire consequences should anyone travel without tickets.

But of course, people did travel without tickets and trouble did erupt; but not in the manner everyone expected. Fans came back from France telling stories of how they had been brutalised by both the French locals and the police, and began to receive a degree of sympathy from the British public. If that sympathy was for football in general rather than the individual, it was sadly misplaced. As the new domestic season began, it quickly became clear that once again there was a massive upsurge in hooligan activity.

As early as 20 August, Norwich and QPR fans were involved in a bottle-throwing battle in a Norfolk pub. In September, 19 people were arrested during the Swindon v Oxford local derby and that same month fighting broke out on a train carrying 200 Manchester United and Coventry City fans to separate fixtures in London. Again in September, 20 Birmingham fans sprayed Norwich fans with CS gas and then attacked them with bar stools in a pub, and in the November, major trouble broke out on a London to Sheffield train which involved fans from Sheffield United, Chesterfield and Nottingham Forest. Attacks on both players and team coaches were also on the increase. Leeds, at both Spurs and Birmingham, and Huddersfield, also at Birmingham, suffered from this as their coaches came under direct attack from fans. In the case of Leeds at Spurs, angry fans even made it onto the coach before the police got them away.

With the police falling way behind in their efforts to contain the trouble, in November 1998 the government announced a consultative document which laid out plans for all kinds of new legislation to counter the growing threat. It was almost certainly designed to influence the 2006 World Cup bid. For those involved in the hooligan scene, the document was merely another challenge to be overcome, though many expressed doubts (wrongly, as it turned out) that these laws would ever come onto the statute books.

If the idea had been to send a warning to those intent on causing trouble, it fell sadly short. For in the quest to stay ahead in the contest with authority, the hooligans had discovered a new weapon: the Internet.

As 1999 arrived, there were approximately eight million subscribers to the web in Britain and many more people had access to it via their workplace. Given that right from the outset a great deal of publicity had been given to the fact that the net could provide access to everything from hardcore pornography to lessons in nuclear bomb building, it should hardly be surprising that people soon began to use it to spread news about football violence. Initially, these consisted of messages posted on some of the more unofficial club pages. But as people became more net-friendly, websites and message boards were set up dealing solely with information and detail about hooliganism that had taken place that weekend. For example, the following was posted on a site the day after Birmingham City visited Bristol City in April 1999:

Yesterday Birmingham City put on an impressive show of force at Bristol City. About 10 minutes into the game, to the sound of 'Zulu Army' from the loyal nonces already in the ground, about 100–150 dressed-up boys sauntered into the seats wearing Stone Island, baseball hats and sunglasses to avoid detection from the CCTV. Bristol had a few boys out and both sides baited each other throughout the game but police had it well sussed with helicopter, dogs and horses – they have been well trained over the years by Bristol's firm. After the game the Zulus were looking to kick things off but were shadowed closely by the police – more a show of force than any serious intent.

Challenges also began to be thrown down, as did invites to 'parties'. A typical example of this is:

Posted by PNE on May 07, 1999 at 12:56:44: STOP PRESS; mob of 60/70 North End expected around Baker St. Can you accommodate DAY OR NIGHT?

The press picked up on this new development for the first time when Millwall travelled to Cardiff in August 1999 and serious trouble broke out. Somehow, the tabloids got hold of the idea that the whole thing had been planned on a certain website and that as the trouble had been going on, a running commentary had been posted for people who were not there. Only part of this was true. What had actually happened was that as soon as the fixtures had been published, people on the web had begun to build up this game, which was always likely to involve trouble given the history of the clubs involved. When it did kick off, a single posting was made on one specific site

The police now went on the offensive. Suddenly, messages started appearing on the main sites asking for specific details or offering information. Anyone who had spent time on these boards realised quite quickly that these were almost certainly being placed by the Old Bill and so bogus messages were sent in return. The problem for the police was that everyone who wrote anything on these sites used a false name and was therefore pretty much anonymous. What is more, possibly as much as 90 per cent of the things posted was (and is) pure bullshit. However, with the police taking an interest, people began to believe that simply logging on to a site could lead to them being identified through their Internet Service Provider. (I am not proficient enough in the workings of computers to know if it would be possible to trace anyone in this way or not, but it would not surprise me one bit if it were.) To counter this concern, some of the more serious hooligans began using cybercafes and even local libraries to send messages. Others simply stopped posting and reverted to more traditional methods.

Despite this, the sites have remained in existence and they all report on trouble that has taken place, although only one regularly includes information about things that are being planned. Increasingly, however, to avoid problems with the police, the trend is to shy away from this kind of discussion and concentrate instead on the background and history of the terrace or Saturday culture.

Discussions revolve not around what happened on Saturday, but what happened at Highbury in 1983 and which bands had links with which club. The fostering of this 'nostalgia' may not present much of a direct problem, but like some of the books that have hit the shelves in recent years, the message boards accompanying these sites tend to talk in rose-tinted terms about what was, and for some still is, a very dangerous and violent time.

While all talk was of the Internet, in the background other changes were taking place. The new legislation was driven through Parliament and when West Ham set out to travel to Metz for the final of the 1999 Inter-Toto Cup, their fans were to learn exactly how powerful these laws were. Two days before they were due to travel, a group of West Ham fans were contacted by the coach company they had booked to take them and were told that the police had put the block on the trip. Despite the fact that the fans all had tickets, the Old Bill claimed that because they had not checked out any of the passengers, permission to take them out of the country had been denied. The fans were obviously furious and a frantic search began for alternative methods of travel. I have been unable to find out if these lads made it to Metz or even if any of them were 'known' to the police. Knowing the area they come from as I do, I suspect police interest in their journey may not have been totally unwarranted.

Yet despite the unhappy start to the season, the autumn and winter of 1999 seems to have witnessed a marked decline in the day-to-day activities of the major hooligan groups. Games with a history of confrontation passed by without incident, and even the mainline stations experienced little or no trouble on what would normally be dangerous days. A good example of this came on 3 October when Leicester were at Spurs, Manchester United were at Chelsea, Arsenal travelled to Upton Park and Leeds United were at Watford. In previous years, the fact that seven major firms were in the capital would have been of serious concern, yet the day was noticeable for an almost total lack of trouble.

To me, this seems to suggest not that the problem is in remission, but that the main players are beginning to realise exactly what is at stake for them as individuals and so they are less reluctant to risk it. Especially on occasions where the police are almost certain to be in close attendance. They will still take part, of course, but well away from the grounds and especially the unwelcome glare of CCTV. If nothing else, this change in attitude also indicates that the scene is beginning to move even further underground than it has been before. This view is reinforced by the emergence of a group of Manchester United hooligans who have begun to carry out their activities wearing SAS-style balaclavas to avoid identification. Although ridiculed by some, this group has already staged a number of hits on rival groups including West Ham in London. This, possibly, is the start of the next phase in the hooligan game.

Because no matter what the police or government do, or what happens on the Internet, football violence can only exist if two people are within touching distance of each other and one of them feels the desire to lash out. While that mentality continues to exist, nothing has really changed since the 1950s or even the 12th century for that matter. And as the game moves into the new millennium, its dark side will continue to fester in the background until the next time it explodes in our faces. That could be next month, next week or even tonight. For me, that is the most frightening thing of all.

Chapter 5
England

This book has thus far concentrated solely on violence within the English domestic league. I have hardly mentioned the game north of the border nor have I tackled in any depth the problems faced when England or English clubs travel abroad. The reason for that is that this book is about hooliganism as it affects the game I watch week in and week out. While the Scots have their problems, as do the Dutch, the Germans, the Russians and even the Americans for that matter, they are *their* problems, not mine; and as such, I don't care about them in quite the same manner – if, to be honest, I care at all.

In the case of the English game, the nature of violence involving my fellow countrymen abroad is totally different from the trouble we see on an average match day at home. It takes on whole new dimensions and often has far greater repercussions, both for the individuals concerned and for the rest of us. As I have said, it is not my intention to go over the history of trouble involving either English clubs or the national side abroad because this was covered in *England, My England*. What I will say is that when we talk about trouble abroad, people must accept right from the outset that club and country are two entirely different issues.

With our clubs, European excursions are simply a continuation of the support we extend back home. The journeys may be longer and the cost greater, but the relationship between the fans and the team is pretty much the same. If anything, it is slightly stronger because even the most apathetic of players will be impressed that supporters have made the effort to travel. But whether we watch our clubs at Norwich or the Nou Camp, generally speaking any trouble still revolves around the actual clubs rather than the country and, as such, the motivation is not essentially xenophobic. There will be plenty of abuse and ridicule, obviously, largely based on stereotypes, for that is one of the attractions of such trips for many people. But support will centre on what good you, as a travelling fan, can do for your team rather than how much you can wind up the natives. Obviously, there will be exceptions to that, but many will be more to do with the history between the two sides than anything else. Certain elements of the Liverpool and Juventus, for example, are hardly likely to get on, in much the same way as either Spurs and Feyenoord or Manchester United and Galatasaray, or Juventus for that matter. Indeed, in 1999, a large group of Juventus supporters took a serious kicking outside Wetherspoons in Manchester city centre.

The national side, however, is a different thing entirely and has two angles, home and away. At home, problems involving England fans are rare and those that do occur usually have more to do with inter-club hostility than anything else. Chelsea and Leeds, for example, have had regular battles in or around the mainline stations of London over the years at England fixtures.

The fact that the majority of international games at Wembley go off relatively trouble-free has more to do with the way the game is run, how the fans are treated and the fact that England play in London than it does with the actions of the Old Bill. For even those involved in hooliganism know when they are getting shafted, and while having it done by your club is one thing, having it done by the FA and Wembley plc is quite another, so many stay away. There is another explanation, of course, and that is that many football fans, myself included, have little interest in the national side because they do not represent me or my team. I would not dream of paying a small fortune to get into Wembley just to see England play a meaningless friendly against some half-arsed side. I'd rather stay at home, watch it on the telly or meet up with my mates and watch it in the pub. Judging by the low attendances for some of those games, I am not alone by any means.

For the big and important games, of course, things are different. People do make an effort because the reputation of the country is at state and even if they can't get a ticket, many will simply travel to London and meet up in Trafalgar Square or the West End. If they are a part of the Saturday scene, they will head for The Globe opposite Baker Street tube station or make their way to Covent Garden. These are the recognised meeting places for the active lads and The Globe, in particular, is widely regarded as being neutral territory. Indeed, in all my times there, I have only ever seen one off. That was during Euro 96 and was a carry-on from a ruck at a domestic game. Showing your face and getting known to your peers is, for many active hooligans, a vital element of their involvement. It is a chance to cultivate both recognition and, more importantly, respect. International fixtures at

Wembley, at least the major ones, provide the ideal opportunity to do it.

The other reason why England sees so little trouble at home is, of course, that no one ever comes and tries it on. Only twice in the last 10 years has a visiting country brought a significant mob who have been up for it. The first was Scotland, who had a fair degree of success during Euro 96. The other was Poland in March 1999 – by all accounts, they brought a very tidy firm of between 80 and 100 lads with them and it was only the close proximity of the police that kept them at bay (that, and what one person who was close by called 'their tactical naivety'). There were rumours afterwards that they were from Gdansk and were actually after some of their compatriots rather than looking to kick it off with the English. But the fact that they came at all was hardly surprising and in terms of boosting their reputation to the rest of the hooligan world, it was a huge success. Some of their more illustrious competitors – Germany, Holland, Italy – have failed to show in recent years, despite ample opportunity and plenty of talk.

When England travel, however, things are entirely different. All kinds of factors come into the equation: fear, bigotry, jingoism, xenophobia and even racism will all make an appearance at some point or another. The problem of hooliganism accompanying the national side abroad is one of the most important aspects of this whole debate, not least because it has the highest media profile and causes the game in this country the most problems both in terms of cost and image. It is also reasonable to assume that for those very reasons, trouble involving England fans employs more time down at New Scotland Yard than any other football-related issue.

Yet despite all of that, and the fact that it has been

going on for over two decades, it continues, seemingly undiminished. The reasons why, as with so many aspects of this debate, are complex and varied. None of them are excuses, of course, but they are reasons nonetheless. For example, one of the things which attracts the most blame for trouble involving football fans abroad is drink (something which applies equally to the tourist industry, as anyone who has spent time in Spain will be only too aware). Yet while we continue to have archaic licensing laws in this country which are totally out of step with the rest of Europe, is it any wonder that people get drunk when they are suddenly exposed to all-day drinking? When I was first posted abroad in the mid 70s, I was pissed for weeks on end. Yet when I finally realised that no one was going to call time and that cheap alcohol would still be available the next day and the day after that, I began to slow down. In the end, I drank less and less to the point where I gave up altogether. In short, I got used to it being available, something you cannot do during a two-week blitz in Benidorm, never mind a 24-hour round trip to Toulouse.

But alcohol, although undoubtedly a factor, isn't wholly to blame for violence involving English football fans abroad. While most people readily accept that a few drinks will liberate their inhibitions, shouldn't we also be looking at what else can be set free? If the circumstances are right, does it also awaken something in our subconscious which most of us are able to keep buried but which others occasionally let loose? For if you sit back and consider this issue with an open mind, there is a case for suggesting that most trouble abroad is caused by one single factor. To some it will be unpalatable, to others it will be offensive. It is certainly contentious but it is most definitely worth thinking about. It has nothing to do with organised firms, the Internet or even the extreme right wing. It is good old English defiance.

Like many people, I am proud to be English. I am not ashamed of where I come from and, as a Falklands veteran, am humbled to have played a part, albeit a very minor one, in the history of this great and glorious country. Sadly, for many years, thanks to the influence of the left-wing do-gooders and the hijacking of the flag by the extreme right wing, that was an unfashionable statement to make. Celebrating England, or Englishness for that matter, was not the done thing. In some quarters it still isn't. But thankfully, due in no small part to the surge of patriotism that surrounded Euro 96, such attitudes are changing. The Cross of St George is no longer regarded as a fascist emblem and despite the efforts of the pro-Europeans and those intent on splitting up the United Kingdom – or maybe even because of them – labelling yourself as English rather than British is no longer regarded as a mortal sin.

Being English, we have a long and distinguished history of accepting abuse, criticism and even ridicule without response. While most of our so-called European partners openly treat us with contempt, and a few regard us with nothing less than outright hatred, we simply turn the other cheek and let them get on with it. Anything else is not the English way, even though in most cases those same nations owe us big time, for their very existence in a few cases. But deep down, we know the truth and are confident enough not to have to argue the toss with people who should show this country both gratitude and respect.

Occasionally, of course, that isn't possible and then, in partnership with the rest of the union and what is left of the Commonwealth, we will rise up and fight back. Once the spirit of John Bull is roused, and the might of middle England gets behind it, it is an awesome, almost unbeatable force. British by birth, English by the grace of God, is how the saying goes. How true.

For the most part, the citizens of this country do not even think about such things. Pride and patriotism are feelings that are best left in the background, to be brought out and dusted off on state occasions, for sporting triumphs or, more usually, when something bad happens. Conflict or tragedy are, sadly, the usual excuses, but the other is when the reputation of England and the English is harmed in some way. More often than not, that means the drunken exploits of our citizens and, more usually, our football hooligans. The sight of yobs in football shirts hurling bottles at the locals or being baton-charged by riot police has brought a degree of shame into almost every home in the country at some point in recent years.

Or has it?

For while our international support has a long, dark history of violence abroad, the truth is that since the 1990 World Cup in Italy, much of that violence has been provoked. Not all of it, admittedly, but certainly most of the major incidents. Although the tabloid press might like to believe that organised riots and hooligan invasions go on, the reality is that, Dublin aside, they do not, at least not to any significant degree. Most fans, even the Saturday lads, travel with England to enjoy the occasion and experience the camaraderie that goes with it. Problems now arise because when England come to town, especially for a tournament, they are preceded by a reputation which, while once richly deserved, is now out of date. Because of that reputation, both the local police and the general public will have been forcefed images of

151

past violence to the extent that they will be expecting trouble, and so will often be far from welcoming and sometimes openly hostile. While this is understandable up to a point, it is no fun being on the receiving end of a reception like that and it is hardly surprising that, occasionally, someone will cry enough is enough and lash out. At which point the local Old Bill will come in mobbed up to try to sort things out. Because of the English reputation, they will immediately blame the visitors – who will respond accordingly. No English lad abroad, especially those involved within the Saturday scene, will stand by and watch while one of their own gets turned over and done down. And so it escalates and before you know it, all hell has broken loose. If it's local lads who are involved, they may well do a runner and things will calm down, but if it's the local police, they will not. They will simply pour more and more men in until sheer weight of numbers brings the incident to an end. But no matter who is involved, the English lads will not back down until they have no choice. They will stand and fight for as long as they are able. In short, they will defend what they perceive to be the honour and reputation of England – and England run from no one.

To understand why that is, maybe we shouldn't look at the individuals who are involved but instead look at those who are not. For while it would be easy to believe that everyone sitting at home watching the evening news would be critical of the fans' behaviour, having talked to many hundreds of people about this very issue over recent years, it has been made clear to me that this is not the case at all. It seems that increasingly, members of the general public are looking at groups of lads strutting arrogantly about in France, Italy or Poland and regarding them not as representatives of English football but rather the subdued spirit of England itself – standing up for themselves and taking shit from no one. I can understand the thinking behind that but I have to say that it genuinely concerns me.

Of all the things I have ever talked about relating to the hooligan issue, this is possibly the most controversial and it is certainly the most provocative. I have no doubt that large numbers of trendy, politically correct journalists will be busily sharpening their poison pencils as I write. Yet if we ever hope to comprehend why it is that England fans are involved in more trouble abroad than most other nations combined, there are questions that must be asked and the answers must be brutally honest. The most obvious question for English people to confront is the accusation that the Scots, in particular, level at us more frequently than any other: that we are arrogant. Do they have a point? Are we, deep down, that conceited that we genuinely believe we are better than anyone else? Take that point a step further and answer the question personally: do you genuinely believe that the hooligans who fight in foreign lands really shame the nation? Or do you gain a degree of smug satisfaction when you watch them causing mayhem on television, and secretly believe that they are doing it on your behalf? Sending the message that no one fucks with the English and if they do, they'll get a good hiding for their trouble. Is that what you think, deep down?

Or maybe it is something else, something even deeper than that. Do we, as many people suggest, resent the fact that we lost an empire? Are we bitter that our credibility and status in the world has diminished, our identity eroded by European interference? Are the English, as many believe, really inherently racist? Not in the sense of prejudice against colour or religion – surely most of us

153

are way beyond that – but in the sense that you're either with us or against us? If that is what you personally think, could the hooligans be the manifestation of that pent-up resentment? Are their actions a last, defiant stand against England's descent into mediocrity?

As I said, they are uncomfortable questions which in many people will have evoked uncomfortable responses. But think back to the scenes in Marseille, as the English lads fought back against all the abuse, antagonism and provocation of the very worst kind, and reflect on your own answers again. Then consider whether it is really so hard to believe that there could just be something in the argument that this behaviour has nothing to do with football at all, but everything to do with the way that the English male is built.

For if this is the reason, or at least one of the primary ones, it would explain why, whenever something does kick off, it involves large numbers of people who are unknown to the police; seemingly average blokes who end up spread across the tabloids or being deported, yet who have no history of involvement in hooliganism at all. What is more, it would also clear up the mystery of why the police have been so ineffective in dealing with this particular aspect of the hooligan issue. After all, how can you legislate or defend against prejudice, latent or otherwise?

It would also partially explain a few more of the problems associated with England fans abroad, the apparent explosion of right-wing extremism among the supporters for one. Most football fans are aware that the right-wing influence is, thankfully, relatively minor these days – indeed, there have been suggestions that the extreme left have had far more success of late – yet when we see travelling England fans giving Nazi salutes and singing anti-IRA songs, many people assume that they are in the majority. Is this because supporters are unwittingly caught up in the xenophobia of the occasion and cannot help themselves? Or are there some who willingly embrace that particular stereotype for the duration of the moment and play up to those images, because they frighten and intimidate? I have spoken to enough individuals who have been involved over the years to suggest that the latter is the more likely of the two. People simply become part-time xenophobics not just because it suits their purpose at that particular time, but because they want to. For many of them it's the only chance they get to show any kind of pride, perverse or otherwise, in their country and their fellow countrymen.

It would, of course, be easy to dismiss the above as the rantings of some right-wing megalomaniac. But that would be missing the point. I have not set out to make any kind of political statement here, nor would I want to. I have no interest in politics other than being pro-football fan. But what I have done is to make an objective examination of a problem that refuses to go away and tried to come up with some kind of explanation. And I have yet to read or hear any other that stands up to any kind of scrutiny.

If, as I suspect and fear, hooliganism involving England fans abroad is dependent on the awakening of various prejudices, then the only way we will ever solve this particular problem is to remove the antagonism and create a welcoming environment for the travelling fans, one in which they, given the inclination, will police themselves. That is exactly how the Scots managed to turn things around to such an extent that these days, host nations cannot wait for the tartan hordes to appear. They do not carry a reputation before them like the English supporters and so are not expected to cause problems for or with the locals. And if anyone does step out of line, then they are swiftly brought to book by one of their fellow country-men. I have asked a number of Scots about this and they have all said pretty much the same thing: that unlike their cousins to the south of Hadrian's Wall, they do not like people besmirching the good name of their country and will not allow it. This, of course, brings us back to the argument about pride, for there can be few nations on this earth more proud of their country than the Scots. But more significantly, unlike the English they are able to openly display that pride and always have been. Can that really be a coincidence?

So how can we arrive at a position where the English are welcomed and treated in the same way, a situation which the vast majority of us would prefer anyway? Initially, as with every other aspect of this problem, the first thing to do is to take a step back and look at it through fresh eyes. Then, having examined the current state of play, we should simply turn it on its head. Rather than prevent England supporters from travelling abroad, we should encourage it.

If England are playing, especially in Europe, football fans will travel in their thousands to watch them. If the team are in a tournament, they will go in their tens of thousands and many will stay for the duration. Most of them, as we saw in France, will have absolutely no chance of getting a ticket through any legitimate source, yet despite that they have to be there. It is like a pilgrimage. The harder you make it for them to travel, the more determined those involved with the Saturday scene are to do it, for they see such obstacles as challenges. Unlike other, law-abiding supporters who may be put off, they will do whatever they can to overcome them.

Therefore, while little can be done to ease the ticket situation, the thing we have to do is not to restrict travel, which is exactly what this government is attempting to do, but to make it easier. For the only way we can ever prove that the majority of English football fans are well-behaved is to make sure that more of them are there to dilute the influence of both the Saturday lads and the part-time xenophobics. If that means the FA funding big screens and setting up tented villages, then so be it. Is it so difficult to believe that, given the opportunity, England fans could export the spirit of Euro 96 rather than the spirit of Dublin?

Such a move, of course, would be a massive gamble, dependent as it would be on the creation of an environment that generates no tension, and could only be done with the assistance of the host nation. Would anyone be prepared to take that risk? Well, it has been tried before: once in Sweden, with no success whatsoever thanks almost entirely to inept policing and poor planning, and once in Germany, where it worked perfectly. The German example should have shown the way forward for the English game, yet sadly, no one took any notice of what they did and how they did it. Only those who were there understood that this was something different and the reaction from the travelling fans was astonishingly positive. The tragedy is, it happened over a decade ago, at the 1988 European Championships.

The idea adopted by the police and citizens of Stuttgart for England's first game was a simple one. They knew that the troublemakers were in a minority and so for once decided to pander not to them but to everyone else. Everything was done in a friendly rather than an oppressive manner. This was an astonishing risk to take given that hooliganism was rife all over Europe during that period, but it was amazingly successful. The provision of a tented and secure village for the England fans to stay in was very well received and the authorities also took the precaution of allocating specific streets for the English lads to gather and drink in, which was a masterstroke. The area surrounding them was heavily patrolled, of course, not just to keep an eye on the England fans but also to keep any local yobs out. Yet fairly quickly, a mutual respect grew between the fans and the police to such an extent that I can remember not a cross word being exchanged between the two. That is not to say there wasn't any trouble, because there was. But it mostly involved local youths and, most importantly, what did happen took place outside these areas.

Unfortunately, the example set by the good people of Stuttgart was not followed at England's next game, nor the one after that. In Dusseldorf, because of the lack of any real provision for those who were camping, many England fans ended up living out of luggage lockers at the railway station, where they came under frequent attack from both German and Dutch fans. As a result, tension rose and it ended up with a serious off during which over 90 England fans and 40 Germans were arrested. Then after the final game against Russia in Frankfurt, 150 English fans were arrested after rampaging through the city centre.

What happened at that tournament proved to me once and for all that if you treat people properly, they will behave accordingly; and if you treat them like shit, you cannot be surprised if they get upset. And when you have barriers provided by both language and culture, that upset all too often manifests itself in abuse and occasionally violence.

If things are ever to change, the start can only come

from the government. For even if we do ever manage to eradicate violence from within the domestic game, the legacy of trouble abroad will continue to haunt England fans wherever they go. We can travel and behave like saints for the next 10 years but we will still be met by apprehension, unease and riot police. Only the government has the power to change that attitude, but to try to do so would, as I have said, be a huge risk. Even I accept that if the fans did travel and were welcomed somewhere with open arms and it still all kicked off, the damage that would do would be irreparable.

Yet surely that is a gamble worth taking. How long can, and should, any government stand by while its citizens are brutalised in the manner we saw in Marseille during the last World Cup? And how long will the majority of football fans who suffer as a result of that treatment allow them to?

By all means clamp down on properly convicted hooligans and stop them travelling, and encourage host nations to hammer those who step out of line abroad, even if that means footing the bill for keeping the thugs in foreign prisons. But the rest deserve better. And after almost two decades of suffering, isn't it about time they were provided for?

Sadly, no matter what action is taken to change attitudes, there are internationals where trouble is inevitable, because there are certain nations whose supporters will never get on. In November 1999, we had the classic example. Not once, but twice. And all within the space of one week.

When England and Scotland were drawn together for the Euro 2000 play-off, talk turned almost immediately to the rivalry between the fans. And with good cause, for the history between them is long and bloody. Two games in quick succession both home and away would give the hooligans the chance to prove once and for all who were the top boys and it rapidly became clear that they had no intention of wasting the opportunity.

Despite a massive police operation, the first game in Glasgow saw a sizeable firm of English hooligans travel. By 2.00, small skirmishes had broken out all over the city but things really kicked off at 3.30, ironically as the game was in progress, when a massive off began in Buchanan Street. This quickly spread and the area saw a number of violent incidents. It took the police until 5.00 to restore calm, and by the time the last of the English fans had left, over 170 people had been arrested.

For the English lads, it had been an overwhelming victory. They had gone to Scotland en masse and basically taken the piss. Yet with another game only days away, it was clear that there was more to come.

As expected, the Scots came to London and gathered in Trafalgar Square while the England fans began to congregate in the pubs around the West End. As dark fell, a large group of them tried to break through the police cordon surrounding the square but were beaten back. Missiles were thrown and, eventually, the police escorted the Scots to Charing Cross tube station where they were put on trains heading for Wembley.

Thankfully, for various reasons, one of which was that as during Euro 96, the English hooligans were totally unorganised, that was the only significant incident of the night. However, there were still a total of 56 injuries and 39 arrests.

But the trouble in Glasgow proved once again that if the circumstances are right, the English hooligans will travel and they will fight. And with Euro 2000 on the horizon, and the potential for trouble with both the Dutch and the Germans, that should be of great concern to us all.

PART THREE
The Authorities

Chapter 6

The Great Game

Recently, I heard someone say that football is now at the stage where it perceives supporters not as a crowd but as a collection of customers. There is some truth in that, although it does miss one essential point. As a 'customer' of any commercial enterprise, I can take my business elsewhere if I am unhappy or certain standards I have every right to expect are not met; but as a football fan, my season-ticket money is destined for only one place, Vicarage Road. I can't take my business elsewhere even if I wanted to because I'm a Watford fan and Watford don't play their home games anywhere else. In short, they have a monopoly on me and my money.

Watford, of course, know that only too well. They realise that they, in common with every other football club, enjoy a special kind of brand loyalty and therefore the price of my season ticket is as good as a fixed asset to them. I will be back next year and the year after that. They don't have to work that hard to keep me happy and on occasions they even seem to go out of their way to exploit that loyalty.

That isn't just Watford, that's every club. What follows is an example of that sent to me by a well-known Chelsea fan who had better remain nameless for fear of retribution from a certain Mr Bates:

As a mere member at Chelsea, I have to buy my tickets to home matches in lumps of six matches in one go (they release them in batches of six matches at a time). The tickets sell out almost immediately, so you *have* to buy six in one go. Most people don't have £144 in cash spare, so it has to be a credit card job. Enter the one pound 'booking fee' for paying by credit card.

I wrote to Ken Bates complaining about it, asking how they could justify charging extra for paying by credit card when it *must* be cheaper for them to do it that way (no large amounts of cash and all the clerical staff and security needed to keep an eye on it). A minion wrote back with platitudes about credit card fraud potentially costing them a fortune, etc. It's all bollocks and amounts to a back-door price increase. Captive market, shit on 'em. Standard business practice.

I buy tickets for six other people and put it all on my credit card. Work it out for yourself: say 20 home matches, not counting Cup games, replays, etc, over the season that's a minimum of 140 tickets that I have to buy, and that means £140 on top of the £24 per ticket.

Now imagine what I'd have to do to avoid paying the booking fee. For the next issue of six games' worth of tickets for seven people, I need to go to the bank, withdraw over £1,000 in cash (I don't have £1,000 in cash), take it to the box office at Chelsea and stuff it under the little window, thus giving every little villain in West London ample opportunity to turn me over on the way into the ground. Chelsea obviously have to employ extra stewards and have police on call for the two days or so it takes to sell all the tickets, so you'd think, would you not, that they'd encourage people to do it by phone, paying by card. 'You can,' they cry, 'but it's one pound extra per ticket.' Ad nauseam.

Football is just about the only large business which still believes that its customers are a necessary but irritating inconvenience. I find it incredibly frustrating.

It is things like this which seem to prove conclusively that in their quest for finance, the clubs have become complacent about the needs of the fans. They think that as long as we get to see the team play and things are going well, that will be enough. For many people it is, but only because they do not consider what it is they actually get in return for their hard-earned, and I am not just talking about quality of football, I am talking about quality of service. In that respect, every professional football club I have ever visited in this country fails miserably. Not because of crap seats, scalding coffee or disgusting toilets, but because of one fundamental reason: safety.

When you walk into a football ground, it is reasonable to assume that the people who administer that stadium have taken adequate provision for your welfare. After all, the law of the land states that it is exactly what they must do and each stadium is granted a safety licence by the Football Licensing Authority to ensure that they comply with the various rules and regulations laid down. There will be people to show you to your seat, provision for the disabled, medical facilities should you require them and even a fireman should the unthinkable happen. In effect, what you will find is exactly the same as you would expect at the theatre or the cinema, with one notable exception. At football, among the paying public will be individuals who will be looking to be abusive and/or violent towards supporters of the other club. As a result, there will be people in the ground with the specific task of making sure that they are unable to do that, at least inside the confines of the stadia.

This is all well and good, and as football fans we have become used to seeing policemen and stewards standing beside the pitch or cameras scanning the crowd for trouble. We have also become used to feeling apprehensive about attending certain away fixtures or walking out of a ground with our head bowed just in case someone takes exception to us. We may have become used to it, but why on earth have we accepted it? More importantly, how have the clubs been allowed to accept it? Not just by us, but by both the football authorities and the law. Because every time a 'known', or for that matter even a suspected hooligan is allowed to walk through a turnstile, it compromises the safety of everyone else. That is totally unacceptable and would not be allowed to continue at any other venue where people pay to be entertained. Yet football gets away with it. Why? Is it because the Football Licensing Authority is reluctant to impose its ultimate sanction or is it that local councils are scared to enforce the law or are afraid of the repercussions? Would McDonald's be allowed to continue trading if their customers routinely caused problems for the locals and the police? Of course not; they'd be closed down or forced to deal with it. This is certainly what happens at pubs and nightclubs. So why not at football?

My own belief is that over the years, football has managed to manoeuvre itself into a position where people are convinced that, as Ted Croker told Margaret Thatcher, hooliganism is not football's problem, it is society's. As a result, it has managed to convince itself that it has no role to play in the search for a solution and has happily abdicated that responsibility, leaving it to the police. Today, many of the people involved in the desperate scurry to stage the 2006 World Cup have become sucked into this fallacy and genuinely believe some of the things they are spouting. Just after France '98, I took part in a radio debate with Sir Geoff Hurst where he stated quite happily that Euro 96 was totally trouble-free. And if someone as well respected as Sir Geoff says it, well, it must be true. So those riots in Trafalgar Square after the games against both Scotland and Germany were obviously a product of my imagination.

The fact that football has worked itself into this position should not come as any kind of surprise because with it having failed dismally to deal with the hooligan issue over the years, it was the logical step to take. If you can't solve a problem, the next best thing is to blame it on someone else. Football sat back and watched while hooliganism exploded in its face in the 60s, could come up with nothing more inventive than caging us in during the 70s, then saw every English club banned from Europe and heard the Prime Minister call into question the very future of the professional game in the 80s. And still it did nothing. It was only after Hillsborough that anything really changed, and that was due entirely to legislation forced on the game by the government. Even then, all we really saw was an influx of money men who suddenly realised there were big bucks to be made if the game, at least at the top end, got off its backside and marketed itself correctly.

Within the top flight, the effect of the Taylor Report on the hooligans' activities *was* major, at least for the clubs, because it forced them out of grounds and into the surrounding areas so that at last, the game could finally justify its claim that the problem was nothing to do with football. Yet still, no one picked up on one simple but indisputable fact; hooliganism only exists because football allows the hooligans to carry out violence and intimidation under the banner of the individual club.

Until the clubs themselves are made to recognise that, the issue of football hooliganism will never be resolved. Football clubs have to accept responsibility for the behaviour of their own fans (or customers), both good and bad, because they reflect the image of both the club and the game to the general public. If those fans step out of line, then the club have to deal with them, as well as the police. And that is far easier than it sounds because football clubs have the ultimate weapon at their disposal: they have the right to deny admittance.

Outside most nightclubs, you will find a sign that says: 'The Management reserve the right to refuse entry.' Usually, this power is enforced by the resident doorman who, if he doesn't like the look of you, will send you on your way. If you do make it past him and step out of line inside, chances are he will throw you out and you will never get back in. It is a simple system and it usually works. So why does it not apply to football? When the resident 'lads' have been going to the same club, have sat or stood in the same place and have been policed by the same stewards and Old Bill for years on end, why are they still allowed in? When every club has a policeman whose role as Football Liaison Officer is to travel with the fans and identify known troublemakers to other police forces, why not simply pass on this information to the clubs as well and tell them not to let these individuals in? No one has a divine right to enter a football ground. It matters not one iota whether you were at Rochdale for an Auto Windshields Cup tie on a Tuesday night six years ago or are a celebrity fan with a free ticket.

Do not have any doubt that it would work, either. If you denied football hooligans the opportunity to attend games at their respective clubs, there is nothing to suggest that they would go elsewhere and nothing to suggest they would still cause trouble. Indeed, there is ample evidence to support the argument that they would simply give it all up. The best example of that can be found in Scotland, where the two big Glasgow clubs solved their own hooligan problems by the use of such a policy. As a result, trouble is rare, although it is making a comeback, largely because the threat has been allowed to slip in recent seasons.

As far as I can see, there is only one reason why this course of action isn't being taken by the clubs: money. It is all well and good putting pressure on Premiership clubs to impose a ban on troublesome supporters – they can afford to lose a few because they will quickly be replaced by new ones. But could smaller clubs, such as Walsall or Bristol Rovers, afford it? Could they risk losing a season's entry money from 10, 15, even 50 lads in the hope that they would be replaced? No, of course not. So club officials continue compromising safety. Not their own, of course, because if that were the case this issue would have been resolved years ago, but that of the rank and file football supporter.

What if one day a fan was assaulted inside a ground by someone they knew to be suspected by the police of being a hooligan and took legal action against the club for failing to protect them? Or even took the local authority to court for granting a safety licence despite the fact that the club were clearly not providing for the safety of the individual concerned? I don't know what the legal position would be, but it sure would rock a few boats if it ever came to court. Any club with a history of trouble could find itself in serious trouble and even, in extreme circumstances, closed down.

The stupid thing is that while the clubs continue to allow these individuals into games, they then have to pay out huge sums to police them. Where is the sense in that?

If all this proves one thing, it is that the people who run our clubs care little for the needs and concerns of the genuine football fan, something which isn't just apparent from their failure to deal with the hooligan question but with any number of issues which have sprung up in recent years. It is somewhat ironic that as supporters, we have to rely on people whose motives for being involved in the game in the first place are often, to say the least, questionable. For example, did they ask us for our opinions when they sold our game to Sky? Did they bollocks. But they still expect us to travel to play our part in the occasion that is the Monday night game on *Sky Sports*. Never mind the fact that we might have to take a day off work to be there or something trivial like that. Or did they ask the supporters when they decided to float their club on the Stock Exchange? No chance. Why bother, when there was so much money to be made by so many directors up and down the country?

Of course, there have been any number of episodes over the years where the clubs have taken decisions which have finally proved too much even for the most loyal of fans to accept. Bond schemes and ground shares are a couple of things that spring to mind, but for me, the one thing that encapsulates the lack of respect clubs have for their fans is the idea of mergers. By their very nature, mergers must involve local clubs and, therefore, local rivals. Can anything be more certain to fire up animosity than the very idea of moving in with your most loathed opponents? Yet we have seen many such proposals over the years. Reading/Oxford and Stoke City/Port Vale are two of the more obvious but an amalgamation between Watford and L*t*n was suggested by some half-wit once. We have even had the chairman of Oldham, Ian Stott, suggesting that his club join with Bury and Rochdale to form Manchester North End. And only recently the idea that the two Sheffield clubs should merge was widely reported. The fact that such a link might make perfect financial, not to mention footballing sense is immaterial. Football is too emotive for common sense ever to enter the equation, and the very fact of such a thing being even considered by a club makes a mockery of its fans' loyalty. Once the supporters start to become disloyal, then the club really has problems. Football fans may know deep down that the people who run our clubs are shafting us, but we don't like having our noses rubbed in it, something events at Newcastle United proved only a couple of seasons ago when two directors learnt first-hand that you do not bite the hand that feeds you.

While our clubs ignore our wishes, the game itself simply treats us with disrespect. Football is funded by the supporters either directly or indirectly, and yet where is our representation? Why is it that the game we fund does not provide us with a platform through which to air our concerns or have our problems resolved? Even Sainsbury's has a customer services department, and what do we get? The Football Supporters' Association. A group funded almost entirely by donations and which, with the best will in the world, has achieved very little in terms of tangible results other than the provision of supporters' embassies at major championships. Do they campaign on your behalf if you have a problem with the stewards at Bradford or the police at Birmingham? Not that I am aware of, and even if they do, would a club really take any notice? If you have such a problem, the only hope for you is to try and get in touch with one of the radio phone-in shows, and hope they will take up your cue. But have they really any power or for that matter interest? Not likely, unless it means increased ratings or more advertising revenue.

We should not be in this position. We should be able to deal with the clubs direct and, if we get no satisfaction, go to the FA and demand it. But we can't because there is no mechanism to do either. That is why we saw the birth of the anarchic fanzine and the spread of the independent supporters' clubs, because they alone provided fans with a platform through which to air their views. All too often those views were ignored, but at least you could get them off your chest.

Aside from the FSA, the other body set up to deal with issues of concern to us is, or should I say was, the Football Task Force. A brilliant idea in principle yet one which was immediately stripped of any credibility when David Mellor was appointed as its head. This so-called 'voice of the fans' is so far removed from the realities of life as a football fan it is shameful, a fact he proves with startling monotony if you ever have the misfortune to hear him on the radio. One of the biggest problems with Mellor was that he seemed so preoccupied with the promotion of David Mellor as an entity that the whole concept of the task force was weakened. He missed many of the regional task force meetings because he had 'prior engagements' and as a result, he failed to win over the fans and, without them on his side, he had nothing. Yet he wasn't the only problem with the task force. To me, of equal significance was its continued obsession with racism and the disabled. Both worthy causes, of course, but does either of these issues impact on each and every football fan? I don't think so, but hooliganism does and if Mellor or any of his cronies had dedicated their time towards trying to put pressure on the FA to stamp out violence in and around our grounds, I would have been the first person to sing their praises. But no, they were too busy trying to work out why there are no Asian players in the Premiership, while the party line on hooliganism was, 'We only do what we are told to do.' Bullshit. Once again, the pursuit of political correctness won the day and it is the majority who suffer as a result.

Of course, we should be used to this and most of us, sadly, are. While we are loyal to our clubs and to the game we love, this is a strictly one-sided affair. The FA are quick to shout about loyalty, tradition and history when it suits them – like when they want to win the right to stage a World Cup or rebuild the national stadium despite our objections – but it's about time they showed some loyalty to us. We are sick and tired of watching our game suffer and it's about time someone did something to sort it out. We are not only talking about the hooligan issue here. For example, the FA needs to deal with people who asset-strip football clubs and then sod off taking huge sums with them, leaving the fans with nothing except the threat of liquidation. Such things are happening to clubs more and more and it is always the rank-and-file fans who have to gather together and save them. That is simply not right. The FA should be making sure that clubs do not get into these situations in the first place.

On the field, things are no better. Players routinely carry out assaults or behave in a manner that would get you or me carted off, or at the very least ejected. We have seen them abusing and even assaulting supporters, and doing things that would have us appearing in court on a charge of incitement to riot. We have seen a massive upsurge in players cheating, a total evaporation of respect for officials and even, down in the non-league game, officials assaulted. Yet all too often they go unpunished either by their clubs or the FA.

The behaviour of players and managers has become one of the most contentious issues surrounding football in recent years. Transgressions or scandals of the kind that would get you or me the sack seem to happen week in and week out, yet come match day they will still be there, out on the pitch in front of the paying public, soaking up the adulation. It is a bad state of affairs which reflects not only on the game and the clubs but on the rest of us. People outside football read about the sordid exploits of players and it reinforces their opinion that the game is played by scum and watched by morons. There appears to be no one to call these players to account.

Furthermore, since the Bosman ruling, the days of player loyalty have all but vanished. Pre-Bosman, players were generally thought of as ordinary blokes doing an extraordinary job. Now they are thought of as pro-fessionals and very highly paid ones at that. Their loyalty to the clubs who pay their wages is only as long as the contract in their pocket, and in some cases it isn't even that long. There are exceptions but, generally speaking, players will turn out for whoever offers them the most money. That's all well and good and fair play to them. After all, we'd all do it given half a chance. But if they want to be thought of, and treated, in a professional manner, then they need to behave like it. They have to set standards of behaviour that reflect both on their employers and their 'fans' and adhere to them. If the players at Watford or anywhere else are pulling in huge sums of money, I expect them to give me 110 per cent for my entrance money every single time. That's all I ask of them on the pitch. What I do not want is to see them appearing on the front pages of the Sunday tabloids. If they do, they could at least apologise for letting us down; and if that's too much to ask then they should be sacked. Pure and simple, just like you or I would be. No pay-offs, no expensive clinics, just handed a P45 and sent on their way. FIFA should put in place a system where if a player was dismissed, his contract would be suspended and remain in force until he found another club and a transfer fee was agreed. That way, the club which acted against him would not lose out too much.

If such a system were put in place, we might finally start to see a return of those old values called pride and respect. Yet sadly, it is unlikely that such a situation will ever exist. In fact, if anything, things are getting worse. Football has now allowed itself to be backed into a corner by money-grabbing agents and finds itself at the stage where players are dictating what clubs they want to play for. Not only that, but the most successful club in the country has been allowed to desert the greatest cup competition in the world for some meaningless pay-per-view television extravaganza. Again, a decision made with little or no regard for the views of the average football fan. In line with most football fans, all I can ask is what the fuck is going on?

On the face of it, such things might have little relevance to the hooligan debate, but in fact their influence is immense. Because if the game ignores the needs and opinions of the average football fan, it breeds resentment, which in turn breeds anger. Then you have friction and occasionally, people will overstep the mark and lash out. Suddenly someone who was wound up by something happening at the club he loves is branded a hooligan. It has happened a thousand times and will continue to do so until the game begins to listen to those of us who hand over our money to watch it. But more importantly, those already involved in hooliganism will feed off this resentment and use it to stir up trouble.

Football has got to address the issue of its relationship with the supporters or it risks alienating us altogether. I believe the place to start is not by spending millions of pounds trying to win us the right to stage the 2006 World Cup, it is by addressing the issue which has haunted the game for over a century and which impacts directly on everyone who watches football in the flesh. Once the game does that, maybe some supporters will begin to think it really does care about what we want rather than how much money it can squeeze out of us.

Yet I doubt that will ever happen. Football has become devoid of any morals and is drowning in a sea of greed. We have too many chairmen whose only interest in their club is what they can take out of it while avoiding having to put anything back in. We have players who I doubt could even spell loyalty never mind explain what it really means, and a game which has allowed itself to become dominated by the whims of an Australian broadcaster. But if ever a situation proved just how rotten things have become, it is the fact that a club I once held dear seems ready to stand by a man who, the day after the FA announced it was throwing its full weight behind the NSPCC campaign to stamp out child abuse, was sent to prison as a convicted sex offender. What kind of message does that send out, not just to children or to parents but to everyone else? How can one club sack a teenager for drug abuse yet another employ a man whose name will be on a sex offenders' register for 10 years? Are people involved in football so desperate for success that they will forgive and forget any indiscretion? I always believed that Watford's signing of the former scummer Kerry Dixon was the worst possible kick in the nuts any club could ever give its own supporters, but this beats that hands down. Not one Chelsea fan I have spoken to is happy with this situation, yet there is nothing they can do about it.

The tragedy for us as supporters is that if any other business treated its customers in this way, they would walk away in disgust. But we don't have that option, because it's football and we love it too much ever to give up on it. Football knows that as well, and that's why it exploits us, patronises us and happily places us at risk of serious injury or worse every time we buy a ticket or push our way through a turnstile. We are forced to sit on the sidelines and look on as the game uses Sky TV money to paper over the obvious cracks, and hope that the day will never come when that money dries up. We all know that day is coming. But as it stands, there's fuck all we, as simple supporters, can do about it.

Chapter 7

The Media

Someone once said that the written word is the most powerful weapon known to man, and they were right. In whatever form it comes, be it written, spoken or even televisual, it has the power to form opinions, change perceptions and build up or destroy individuals. Having such power at your disposal is an awesome responsibility and as such, writers, be they authors or journalists, have a duty to stand by every single word they create. As someone who writes things that many people regard as controversial, it is something I have to bear in mind every time I switch on my computer.

Any power I have is generally limited to what I am able to put into a book, and those books are infrequent. However, newspapers come out each day while news is broadcast continuously. The power the media have is immense, but where you have power, inevitably you will get some who will abuse it. People will write things that are pure fabrication and pass them off as truth, while others will simply twist facts to conceal reality. Worse than that, some will consciously construct stories to try to mould opinion to suit their own ideals or objectives. When those objectives involve the destruction of an individual's reputation, then it isn't hard to see how a few basic 'errors' can quite easily cause irreparable damage.

I know, because I have been the victim of such action not just once, but numerous times.

Thankfully, I am the kind of person who can shrug off such stuff secure in the knowledge that I know it's crap, and I always have the option of writing another book and responding in kind. But others are not so strong. Reputations, careers and even lives have been destroyed by the media in the past and while some people deserve it, others do not. For the average Joe, if the media get on your case, it's all over; mud sticks. If you harp on about something long enough and remain unchallenged, eventually people will begin to believe it. Hooliganism is a case in point.

While the history of hooliganism is one of abject shame both for those involved and for the authorities, the role the press has played is far from honourable either. Indeed, it can be argued with some justification that the press were largely responsible for the explosion of hooliganism in the late 50s and early 60s. By sensationalising it in the way they did, they made it sound attractive to an element of British youth who, at that time, were already experiencing a cultural rebellion of sorts. The beaches of Brighton may have been the battleground for the Mods and Rockers, but the football grounds quickly became the arena for most of the others.

As things got worse, football fans began to aspire to reading about their own exploits not just in the regional press but also in the national papers. The press, of course, were happy to fulfil that desire, publishing weekly reports of terrace violence, often accompanied by graphic photographs, to satisfy a hungry market.

In 1974, with the tabloids searching for new ways to cover the issue, one of them printed a league table showing who were the worst behaved supporters in the country. Manchester United were at the bottom of that table by over 100 arrests. Within days, fans from other clubs had set out to take that title. Trouble at grounds became even more widespread and the other papers quickly latched on to what was happening (when the table next appeared, it had been reversed, with the worst club at the top).

By the time the BBC showed the infamous edition of *Panorama* in 1977, which as we have seen detailed the exploits of Millwall's F-Troop, the hooligans' impact on football was already immense. This programme made things even worse. Clubs from Carlisle to Exeter now wanted their own versions of F-Troop. It was one of the major factors in the spread of hooliganism at that time. There have been many more such examples since, but there is a simple point to be made here: the British press love football hooliganism.

Hooliganism provides everything a good story should have: drama, tension, fear and villains. Throw in a bit of shame and the odd pinch of xenophobia and you have the lot. In a responsible climate, the press would be full of condemnation and demanding action from the authorities. We have had plenty of the condemnation over the years, but little in the way of action. Because when you have something like football violence, which explodes onto the scene every so often and makes great copy, why on earth would you want to try to stop it?

As someone who does a lot of work with the media, I can understand the thinking behind that. To most journalists, often under extreme pressure to get exactly what their editors want, a story is just a story. The subject is, in the main, immaterial and once that story has been filed, it's forgotten. Yet when supplying that story includes the spreading of misinformation or, worse, downright lies, then that is unacceptable. It is an abuse of the ultimate power the media hold, which is the power to shape opinion.

In the context of the hooligan debate, it is an inescapable fact that such practices go on in news organisations. For example, if you see film of football fans rioting while someone is talking about English hooligans, it is reasonable to assume that the film and the words relate to each other. Similarly, if you see film of riot police steaming in and hammering groups of men wearing England shirts while the talk is of the disgrace this has brought on the country, then the obvious assumption is that the England fans are to blame. Yet if the film is of foreign fans causing trouble, and it is the riot police doing the attacking, who is there to make the distinction for the viewers? More often than not, no one. And so these 'facts' are put on display to the public, who sit in their front room and put two and two together to come up with a healthy five. And once an opinion is formed, it is incredibly hard to change it.

Such things and more have happened within the last few years. For example, in 1997, just before the last World Cup, England travelled to Rome and trouble erupted inside the stadium. The riot police gave the fans inside the ground shit and for about two hours the TV and radio were going mad saying that the England fans were getting exactly what they deserved. Then, someone realised that the area of the ground involved was full of corporate clients and, more importantly, celebrities. These included, among others, David Mellor's son. Almost immediately, the tone of the reporting changed and it was 'bastard Italian policemen' who were the disgrace. A total turn-around. Yet had no one realised the mistake, the reporting would have continued to be an attack on the England fans, with the result that opinions were hardened and good work undone.

Another instance of this came in Marseille during France '98. England fans found themselves caught in the middle of civil unrest and ended up fighting for their lives on the beach while the French police stood by and did nothing to help the women and children caught up in it all. Yes, there were some England fans there who were looking for trouble and, indeed, who caused plenty. But most were there purely for the football, yet the British press labelled them all as one entity and heaped the blame on them – until the howls of protest became so loud that even they realised the mistake they were making.

There has also been a great deal of concern in recent years about the way the media hype up the problem of hooliganism to the point where they actually provoke it. With Euro 96, they spent months during the build-up to the tournament telling us that every hooligan group in Europe would cross the Channel to take on the locals. There was page after page of photographs showing Danes, Germans, Dutch and even Scottish lads all raring to come over and kick some English arse. Most of these stories, as anyone who knew anything about hooliganism realised only too well, were utter bollocks. Yet by the time the tournament arrived, Mr and Mrs Average were convinced that World War Three was imminent and, more importantly, the English lads were fired up. Talk became not of if but when. If that wasn't incitement, then I don't know what is.

Of course, while the press seem increasingly happy to do this, they are not the ones who have to suffer the consequences. The police and publicans usually end up in the front line, often in front of a camera crew or three. What follows is an extract from a letter sent to me by Paul, a publican from Bognor Regis. It refers to Euro 96 but is just as relevant to any other tournament England or an English club are involved in.

Bognor is a non-footballing town really, and even though England had just drawn with Switzerland, no one seemed to be paying that much attention to what was happening. Then we beat the Jocks and humiliated Holland and it all started. The press were going mad in the build-up to the game against Spain, all that Spanish Armada and Francis Drake rubbish. It was front page stuff in some of the tabloids, really winding everyone up and suddenly, the town is buzzing.

England win and everyone pours out of the local pubs and starts dancing in the street, then on cars, and eventually the trouble started. A police car was rolled onto its side and then they tried to do the same to a double-decker bus with women and kids on board.

Working in a pub with no TVs in, we get to hear all the trouble and then we started to get it first-hand. Locals, regulars who have been impeccably behaved for years, suddenly start pissing in the beer garden and throwing pints over each other. Everyone seemed to become an instant arsehole and that was just the game that put us into the semis.

The night of the Germany game was worse. The papers had been at it again, stirring up the old 'we'll

fight 'em on the beaches' stuff and it was obvious
that if we lost, all hell would break loose. Which, of
course, is exactly what happened. Again, we had
no telly in the bar and so for most of the night it had
been like a morgue. I think we'd had something like
four customers up until 10.25, and they were all
women. But at 10.30 it was 300. All singing, shouting
and swearing. Within about 10 minutes we'd had
two fights, one in the toilets and one on the patio,
and then the police turned up. But the crowd outside
just told them to fuck off and they did.

How we got through the rest of that night I don't
know, but we were lucky. A pub up the road which
had shown the game on a big screen took £2,000
across the bar but suffered £3,000 in damages. At
another pub, they had a 60-man brawl out the front.

Occasionally, members of the press do not even bother
to hunt for a story; they simply stage it themselves. Tales
of journalists paying for photographs of lads fighting or
making obscene gestures are the norm when England
travel abroad. I first came across this in Germany when
England were there in the late 80s, but it isn't just English
journalists who indulge in this practice. I was recently
told of a French reporter who offered some English lads
a few hundred francs to burn a French flag during the
last World Cup so that he could get a photograph. Thankfully, the lads he asked declined his offer (primarily
because two of them were policemen!) but others will
have taken it up and in the end, the reporter will have
got what he wanted.

The fact that the media are able, and quite often happy
to put across these images or this misinformation and
portray them as fact is of serious concern, as is the fact

that they are never held to account for it. The reason for that, especially in the context of football, is that it has been going on for so long now that it has become almost acceptable practice. You only have to look at most of the transfer speculation that gets written up as 'exclusive' to see that. Most of it is, after all, pure bullshit.

I want hooliganism reported because I believe that people have to know what is going on, but I want it reported sensibly. And the media have a responsibility to provide that. For the last 30 years or so, that is something they have all too often failed to accept.

Yet this is only a part of the problem. The media have other questions to answer because every so often, they sneak in something that paints hooliganism not as a negative but as a positive. Over the last few years, we have seen active hooligans feted almost as 'anti-heroes' and treated like celebrities, while videos of football violence have been put on general release and marketed as 'action-packed'. We have also seen articles in magazines which paint a glowing picture of life among the lads. In the spring of 1999, one particular magazine published an article written by a reporter who had travelled to Manchester City with a group of Millwall fans for the league clash we examined earlier. If that piece was supposed to be critical of the hooligan culture, then it fell short by several miles. Words such as 'euphoric', 'rush' and 'buoyant' peppered the article and while I can understand the reporter getting caught up in the intensity of it, there is no excuse for the article being published in the form it was. It was as good an endorsement of being a part of a firm as you are likely to read.

I realise I am being unfair here. Just as football fans are regarded as a single entity, so I am making the same mistake. There are hundreds, even thousands, of decent, hard-working journalists who would never dream of doing anything which they would regard as unethical. And just as football has to live with the curse of hooliganism, so the press have to stick with the negative public perception of them and their profession. Nor should we forget that while it is journalists who construct the stories, in many cases they are dependent on research and quotes supplied by others. There are plenty of people who will happily supply an inflammatory sentence or two if asked or, better still, paid – something I, in my earlier days, was guilty of on many occasions.

It is also fair to say that to a certain extent, the press are in a no-win situation when it comes to hooliganism. If they give it too much coverage, they are accused of glamorising it; too little and they are ignoring it. Indeed, there have been stories floating around for years that the press are a part of some conspiracy to cover up the problem of football violence. Somewhat bizarrely, I first heard this theory during the build-up to Euro 96 when, to my mind, the papers were full of football hooliganism.

The latest version is that the media, together with the FA and the police, are party to a government inspired cover-up designed to win us the 2006 World Cup. This story, which was most recently given a long airing in *When Saturday Comes*, is so ridiculous that it beggars belief. Where were these people during the last World Cup? Did they not see the acres of newsprint or watch the hours of news coverage on the TV? In the two days after the trouble in Marseille, I did 32 interviews, 15 of them on television. In France you couldn't help but have tripped over the legions of reporters and film crews desperately searching for stories about organised firms and 'Category C' thugs. And that was just during the tournament itself. The build-up to it, with all the talk of potential mayhem, bordered on hysterical. When the emergence of the so-called 'cyber-thug' came to the attention of the tabloids in August 1999 following the trouble in Cardiff, the press were equally manic, with the result that widespread coverage was given to the problem once again. I know the FA are inept sometimes, but if they were looking to cover anything up, even they could have put together a better job of it than that.

There is no cover-up. What happens is simply that a story about Mob A smashing up a pub where Mob B were drinking may well fill the local papers but in national terms it is simply one of many similar incidents and just isn't worthy of valuable space. However, when you have a story such as Dublin, a major tournament like the World Cup or the death of a fan such as at Gillingham in 1997, all hell breaks loose. Suddenly it's big news and it's everywhere, but only because something has happened to spark interest in it. That isn't just unique to hooliganism, either. Look at stories relating to dog attacks on kids as another example. Every so often you will get a serious one and then you'll get a spate of them reported. The reality, as any journalist could tell you, is that they happen all the time. It just needs one big one to kick off media interest.

However, because football violence does receive so little coverage in the national media, it allows the FA to tell everyone that there is no hooliganism any more. And all the while, the police continue to send huge bills to every football club in the land for anti-hooligan security!

Before I begin to sound too sympathetic towards the media, what they should be held to account for is the hypocrisy of their coverage. They condemn the hooligans for what they do, yet it is they themselves who hold the power to force a solution. I am convinced that if one of the tabloids staged a concerted offensive against the FA and the clubs and demanded action, then we would see something positive being done to eradicate hooliganism for good. The press have that power at their disposal, yet it remains unused. As I have said, perhaps football hooliganism is just too invaluable a source of news.

Once in a while, however, the media do get it right, showing how they can shape the opinions of the sporting public for the better. The greatest example of this sadly doesn't involve football, but cricket. It also explains the reason for the title of this book, for it offers a glimpse of how things really could change for the better.

When groups of people began following the England cricket team around the globe, they quickly developed a reputation for being different from the average English cricket lover; more Kingston, Jamaica, than Kingston-upon-Thames. They caused a great deal of unease at first but managed to forge themselves a reputation as loveable rogues who simply loved to get drunk and make loads of noise. Eventually, a grateful media latched on to the idea and awarded them almost celebrity status. Eventually, the cricket establishment was forced, albeit grudgingly, to accept them. They became almost a mascot for the national side and were eventually labelled 'The Barmy Army'. As a result of the positive media coverage they continue to receive, when the England cricket team travel abroad there will be nothing written about how many riot police will be required but plenty about how much beer the Barmy Army will drink.

To me, what has happened here is nothing short of astonishing. Thanks to the efforts of a few people, cricket now has what football should and could have. In effect, it's hooliganism without the violence and intimidation.

The noise and passion are there in bucketloads but it's all done in a good-natured and relaxed atmosphere. Cricket's Barmy Army have become almost a sideshow to the main event.

But if you take a closer look at them, many of them are wearing football shirts. Yet they do not step over that line and adopt the culture of hatred we see inside football grounds because the media, by portraying cricket's Barmy Army in a good and positive light, as rascals rather than yobs, have ensured that the public regard them not as a threat but with something bordering on affection. Just as importantly, the Barmy Army perceive themselves in the same way. They regard themselves as an asset, one to be at worst tolerated and at best applauded. They do not receive the attention from the local police that football fans do, and so don't feel intimidated. Therefore, they feel no desire to intimidate in return. With cricket's Barmy Army there is just enjoyment, humour and passion. Cricket should go down on its bended knees and thank the media for that, because if they had covered the Barmy Army differently from the start, irreparable damage could have been done to the sport.

As a football fan, I know that the real Barmy Army follows football. But sadly, because of the continued existence of the hooligan minority, our particular Barmy Army will almost certainly never be regarded with anything approaching the same kind of affection as our cricket-loving brethren. To me, as someone who was once among that minority and as such must take my share of the blame, that is devastating.

If things are ever going to change, then we must accept that we cannot rely on either the game or the clubs to do anything unless they are given a major kick up the arse. They have the ultimate power to deal with this problem but in the past, football has only ever been forced into action following tragedies such as Heysel or Hillsborough, and we should not have to wait around for more people to die before something is done. Therefore, until supporters get themselves organised and have a coherent, fully representative and effective group to state our case, the only people with the power to apply the size nines are the media. If the members of the press suddenly decided that the 99.9 per cent of supporters deserved better than to be infected with this cancer, football would be pummelled into action. Sadly, given their history and their love-hate relationship with the hooligans, I wouldn't place any money on them doing up their laces just yet.

Chapter 8

The Academic Approach

_____

As anyone who has ever asked me will know only too well, my regard for the majority of academics who profess to 'study' hooliganism can be summed up in a few very short, well-chosen words. Suffice to say that I do not hold most of them in very high esteem.

The reasons for my prejudice are many and varied. Some, admittedly, are down to personalities, but they are not the main problem. My belief is that, in common with a number of other bodies involved with the hooliganism issue, the academics are not actually that keen on searching for a solution. Although they will contest that until they are blue in the face, I have enough evidence here in my office to convince me it is true. What's more, this same evidence seems to explain why that should be.

On a shelf here, I have a folder. As I write this, it is 18 months old and inside are letters from various people, both male and female, who all ask me for the same thing: information. The requests range from background detail on the spread of CCTV to the influence the mobile phone has had on the organised hooligan mobs, and all these requests have two things in common. The first is that none of them were accompanied by a stamp and, as a result, were never replied to (after all, if you want something from me, why should I pay to give it to you?). The second is that they are all from students. At the last count, there were over 80 of these letters and they arrive with monotonous regularity.

While these letters are an irritation, they also show conclusively that the study of hooliganism, or to be more anal, hooligan-related issues, has become one of the growth areas in the world of academia in recent times. Quite a respectable little cottage industry has been constructed around it, one which provides employment to a good number of academics. Inevitably, those people are fiercely defensive of what they do and what they have. And why not? This is a job that provides many of its workers with travel around the world to watch football and a decent wage into the bargain – and all in the name of research. On top of that, they are afforded great kudos and are frequently feted by the media for whom, in return, they provide quote after quote after quote. Who in their right mind wouldn't want that, and what wouldn't they do to keep it?

What we have here is actually just a conveyor belt that simply churns out more and more academics, many of whom have been schooled in theories which offer a cross between the blindingly obvious and the downright bizarre. For example, those who ally themselves to Marxist theory have in the past explained away hooliganism as a result of working-class football fans setting out to recapture the game from middle-class infiltration; while John Williams, head of the Sir Norman Chester Institute, once noted without a trace of irony that when he travelled abroad with English fans, the same faces kept cropping up. I wonder how much that pearl of wisdom cost the British taxpayer?

Those who have been taught these theories will, almost inevitably, regurgitate them at some point. And if, as seems the norm, they become teachers – what else can an anthropologist do except teach another anthropologist? – you have a never-ending cycle of bullshit which is never challenged unless it is by another academic who merely replaces it with another, even more outlandish notion. And that is the whole crux of the matter. For apart from new recruits, just what does this industry produce? The answer, quite clearly, is nothing.

In the normal scheme of things, that would be great, for them at least, and need not bother the rest of us. But although their theories are rarely, if ever, acted upon, the fact that they come from professor this or doctor that gives them an air of credibility and some people, especially our more gullible Members of Parliament, take them as gospel and spout them off whenever they get in front of a camera. Then you get problems; because what started out as some half-brained idea suddenly ends up forming policy – and that affects us all.

The man at the forefront of the academics' love affair with hooliganism is the aforementioned John Williams, a sociologist who first came to the attention of the footballing world in the early 80s when his name appeared on the front of work with such evocative titles as *If You Think You're Hard Enough . . .* and *The Social Roots of Football Hooligan Violence*. But it really came to the fore in April 1984 when he, together with Eric Dunning and Patrick Murphy, published a book called *Hooligans Abroad*. It is actually quite an interesting read, if only because it shows just how much you can get away with if you do it in the name of 'research'. For example, at the core of this book are a number of 'revelations' such as the majority of football hooligans come from working-class backgrounds, live on council estates and play unsupervised from an early age. Quite possibly one of the greatest 'catch-all' statements ever put into print.

But that wasn't the only bombshell John had for us. Not only had he and the others done all this 'research', he had actually witnessed football violence in the flesh. Using a system he called 'Disguised Participant Observation', but which I prefer to call 'Watching From As Far Away As Possible', Williams had 'studied' the hooligans at Leicester City and now claimed to understand what hooliganism was all about and why these men did what they did. This, in turn, led him to construct various proposals designed to stop hooligans travelling abroad with either their domestic side or the national team. These proposals make for an absorbing, if slightly humorous read. They include such intriguing ideas as making football fans travel abroad on coaches because they are more easily supervised, and the formation of a special group of FA-appointed stewards to travel with those fans. Strangely, despite the fact that the then chairman of the Football Association, Bert Millichip, was quoted as saying he had read this book not once but many times, policy was not changed as a result.

But even though Bert wasn't sufficiently impressed to act on anything, quite a lot of fuss was made about this book at the time and Williams quickly found himself elevated to almost celebrity status, especially among his peers. So much so that in 1987, when Sir Norman Chester founded his institute for football research, John's was one of the first names on his list. What's more, it seems that much of the work carried out by the centre revolved around theories Williams had first produced and so he suddenly became an integral part of the policy-making process.

From then on, John Williams became a kind of rent-a-quote for anything to do with football hooliganism and as the leading academic in his field, his work went pretty much unchallenged. But there was a cloud on the horizon and it arrived right over John Williams' head in March 1996. For that was when *Everywhere We Go* was first published.

Suddenly, not only was there someone seriously questioning the things he was coming out with, but they were also critical of his methods. John's answer to this, despite the fact that Euro 96 was imminent, was to all but vanish. He was clearly not best pleased.

As time passed, he crept back onto the scene and then, in November 1997, went on the offensive. *When Saturday Comes* gave him two pages with which to rip into my co-author and me. Eighteen months later, both John and *WSC* were at it again. This time we were 'grisly' and 'furiously monotonous', while our books were being marketed under a spurious 'clean-up football' motif. If they were expecting a reaction, at least from me, it never came, except that when I read the magazine while standing in WH Smith (well, I'm hardly likely to buy it, am I?) I simply laughed out loud.

My thoughts on John Williams are hardly the most supportive he will ever hear, but it would be wrong of me to blame him alone for the failure of the academics to deliver anything remotely resembling a solution to the hooligan problem. There were many before he came along, some of whom were responsible for coming up with the stereotypes we still know and hate today. The good old 'right-wing, broken home, product of Thatcher's Britain' mantra which, in many cases, certainly my own, actually aided hooligans as they carried out their activities because the police worked to those stereotypes and if you didn't fit them, how could you be guilty? In this respect, the blind faith shown in the early 80s by both the government and the FA in the academic approach to the hooligan issue actually sustained the growth of it.

Sadly, there is little to suggest that anyone has learnt the lessons of the past and money is still heaped on organisations such as the Sir Norman Chester Institute every year. That, to me, is frighteningly narrow-minded and is proof that those charged with running the game on our behalf are scared to admit their mistakes and reluctant to explore new avenues in their search for a solution to the problem.

I have said it before, and I will say it again: the only person who can truly explain why grown men get off on steaming into a pub full of opposing fans and kicking off trouble is someone who has done it. It is not someone who uses 'Disguised Participant Observation'. They may have studied and observed but have they enlightened and come up with possible solutions? The answer in both cases is no. And that says it all.

Chapter 9

The Police

Many years ago, I was on a football special as it pulled into Birmingham's New Street station. As we stepped off the train, the usual singing and shouting began and increased in volume as we shuffled along the platform towards the station concourse. In front of us stood a long line of the West Midlands' finest and as we approached, this huge copper leant over the barrier and for no apparent reason, grabbed one of the lads I was with and dragged him over. He lifted him up off the ground by his collar until their faces were just inches apart and screamed, 'You're in Birmingham now, you little cunt, no fucking singing!' before shoving him back over at us. I have never forgotten that and although I had already seen enough evidence over the years to support the widely held view among football fans that all coppers were bastards, that was the thing that clinched it for me.

Nothing I have seen or heard since has done anything to change that attitude, at least not in terms of their role at football. Furthermore, the catalogue of incidents I have both witnessed and experienced which bear testimony to that opinion would fill a book on their own. They range from lads being thrown out of games for no apparent reason to watching helplessly while a good mate of mine was treated in a manner which I would not expect to witness in a South American dictatorship. I have seen a vanload of policemen ignore a group of thugs battering the shit out of some poor scarfer not 10 yards away from them, and cowered in a shop doorway while a group of uniformed animals ran past me laughing while they baton-charged a bunch of totally innocent supporters. I have stood in the dock as a defence witness for a mate who was arrested and charged with threatening behaviour towards me (work that one out), and listened while an officer of the law stood in court and lied through his teeth about an incident I actually witnessed. Where the police are concerned, I am not, as you can appreciate, a fan.

There will be many people reading this book who feel the same as I do, which is a sad indictment of the police and their general attitude to football and its fans. But someone once argued that a nation gets the police force it deserves and if ever anything supported that statement, it is football. Yes, some policemen are bastards, but so are some football fans. And over the years, just as my opinion of them has become jaundiced, sure as eggs are eggs, some of them will feel the same way about us.

The fact that many football fans, and in particular the hooligans, regard the police as the enemy is one of the key problems we will need to overcome if we are ever to resolve the issue of football violence. Yet my belief is that it is not the duty of the police to deliver that solution. They are present at games to ensure the safety of the general public and are responsible for dealing with those who wish to cause trouble. But they cannot be expected to change the attitude of those who wish to cause that trouble, nor modify the culture that allows them to exist. The responsibility for that lies elsewhere.

Just as the nature and execution of football violence has changed over the years, so has the way the individuals responsible for that violence are policed. Where once the mere sight of a copper's uniform was enough to calm a situation, these days often the reverse is true. Indeed, the arrival, and sometimes even the behaviour of the boys in blue frequently cause more problems than it could ever hope to solve.

Part of the reason for that is that the competition with the police has developed into one of the most important aspects of the hooligans' game. For some, it is the most important aspect of all. The police have always been aware of this. They also know that those who are intent on causing trouble have always had an unwritten rule book, a kind of hooligans' code of honour, if you like, and part of that code used to be that if the Old Bill got hold of you, you took whatever came your way without complaint. The police used to take advantage of this quite regularly, especially back in the 70s and early 80s when a number of forces would frequently administer their own particular brand of instant 'justice'. In my very early days as a fan at Chelsea, there were strong rumours that the police had a blue Transit which was used specifically for 'sentencing'. Play up and get pulled and it was court or a kicking, the choice was yours. For many, a swift hiding in the back of a van was infinitely preferable to ending up in the clock.

Whether this was true or not is difficult to confirm, but what I can say is that I have heard similar stories over the years about numerous forces around the country who indulged in this practice, using any number of methods.

Not all of them involved actual violence, either. One such example was told to me by a fan from Liverpool called Nick.

I was about 14 at the time so it must have been '78 or '79, but I know it was in the winter because it was dark when we came out of the ground. A load of us were standing on this corner waiting for the opposition lads to show when the bizzies turned up and started giving us grief. Me being only a kid, lipped them back and before I knew it, that was it, I was in the van and away. They drove around for a while and every so often would stop and throw someone else in with me until in the end there were about six of us. I knew a few of them, I think the oldest was about 16, but we were all cold and really pissed off.

Well, next thing I know, the doors fly open and this copper gets in and tells us to take off our shoes. Well, we told him to eff off and so he whacks the lad nearest him across the shins with his truncheon. Fuck that, I thought, and so I took mine off like a shot and so did the others. The bizzie picks them all up, climbs out and next thing we know, we're off again.

So by now it's about 7.30 and it's fucking dark out. The van's still driving around and none of us knew where we were when all of a sudden, it stops. Then the door flies open and the bizzie tells us to get out. We're only on the fucking docks, aren't we, stood there with no shoes on, in the freezing cold and in the pitch black. One of the lads asks what the fuck is going on and the copper just laughs, lobs all our shoes into the water and then gets back in the van and they fucked off.

So we're just left there. It's so dark, I can't even see my shoes in the water even if I wanted to go in and get them, and so all we could do was walk home. I tell you, that was the longest and scariest walk of my life. Can you imagine how fucking scary a dockyard is at night when you're 14? As if that wasn't bad enough, my old man gave me a right hiding when I got home because I had to tell him I'd lost my shoes. I couldn't tell him the truth, could I?

Still, it taught me a lesson, that's for sure. Never gob off at the bizzies.

Another example of this type of 'justice' comes from Gary, a fan from Islington.

We were up at Villa. As usual, we'd been really mouthy to the locals and a few of the lads had been giving the Old Bill some stick as well. Now in those days, they didn't piss about up there and you could see that some of them were getting the right hump with us, so I left it out and moved away a bit. Anyway, the second half starts and something happened on the pitch, I can't remember what, and I steams down the front and starts giving their players shit. Next thing I know, I've got Old Bill all over me and they're dragging me out.

Now I thought I'd just get thrown out but instead, they walked me right round the ground and slung me out at the Villa end. Usually, that would have been bad enough, but as this copper pushed me out, he shouts out as loud as he could, 'Now fuck off home, you Cockney cunt.' Then he slammed the door. Now I look up and what's across the road but about 10 Villa lads who, from the look of them, had also been slung out. Mind you, if they were pissed off, seeing me cheered them up at a stroke.

I tell you, I ran for fucking miles before they gave up. That bastard copper set me up. No question.

Often, back in those heady times, the police weren't so discreet. Tactics such as running individuals down terracing at speed and then letting them go or even tripping them up so that they fell heavily were frequently employed, as was the practice of detaining people and releasing them without charge once games had finished or specials or coaches had left, something which caused incredible inconvenience. It has to be said, though, that more often than not the people treated in this manner deserved it. They were, after all, a major pain in the arse and were busily dragging the game down week by week. But occasionally, this instant justice was arbitrary and random. Victims were selected not on the basis of guilt but because they were easy to get to or simply easier to handle.

These days, of course, things are very different. The police no longer have to rely on the administration of instant justice – which is not to say they do not use it on occasions – because they have an astonishing array of both technological and legal back-up at their disposal with which to combat the hooligan menace. Today, if you step out of line inside a ground, you can be spotted on CCTV, arrested a few days later and charged in court with an offence from the Football (Offences) Act 1991. Even if you didn't receive a custodial sentence, you would almost certainly become a feature on the National Criminal Intelligence Service (NCIS) records and may even be awarded 'Category C' status, meaning you could face restrictions if you wanted to travel abroad with either your club or your country. And as you travelled around England, your face would be a regular feature of pre-match briefings and every copper you saw on match day would know who, and what, you were. If things develop in the way that they seem to be, you could even lose your job.

Cause trouble outside a ground and matters are less likely to take this path, because the chances of getting identified are fairly remote. But not for long. A system known as Mandrake has already been trailed in Newham, East London, and also at Vicarage Road. It is, in effect, a computerised face recognition system which can scan a crowd and instantly pick out anyone on any computer linked to it. Big brother is almost upon us, because this system would enable the Old Bill to track the movements of individuals and mobs who are already known to them, as well as of individuals they might be 'interested' in. The civil liberties implications of this are immense, but the police counter the idea of such a system with the obvious point: 'If you've done nothing wrong, then you have nothing to worry about.' And if you are a victim, then such a system could well bring your attacker to book quite quickly. Whether this is a strong enough case to justify it has to be a matter for personal judgement.

With technology moving so rapidly, new equipment is being devised and tested all the time. Already, at Millwall, we have seen trials of equipment designed to eavesdrop on what supporters are saying, and now we have the ultimate concept, the policeman with a video camera in his hat. Ridiculous though this sounds, the idea has been floated for many years and I have heard of it being trailed on both dogs and horses. Cleveland police have already tried it out at Middlesbrough with remarkable success. Have no doubt, it will be coming to a ground near you within months.

As if all this technology wasn't enough, the police have now been handed a whole new batch of laws with which to combat the threat of hooliganism. Already at their disposal are the Sporting Events (Control of Alcohol, etc) Act 1985, the Public Order Act 1986, the Football Spectators Act 1989 and the Football (Offences) Act 1991, all of which are either totally devoted to the control of football fans or contain elements that are. Yet seemingly, that wasn't enough. In November 1998, the government launched a document called *The Review of Football-Related Legislation* which put forward 29 recommendations. Some were designed to deal with various loopholes in existing legislation, such as being unable to convict an individual chanting racist abuse, while others were more speculative, such as the removal of an individual's passport on 'suspicion'. Amazingly, when they issued the document, the government actually asked for supporters to respond and gave us a deadline of 26 February 1999. However, while many of us were still scribbling furiously, a backbench Tory MP, Simon Burns, who by his own admission was not a football fan (although within a few days he had developed a sudden affinity for Manchester United) appeared from nowhere and published a Private Member's Bill which, bizarrely, included almost every recommendation included in the review. His bill received huge support from every minister in the Cabinet and rendered the whole 'consultative' process utterly pointless. Fans' concerns about specific points were all but ignored while other (obviously more important) voices were taken on board. The best example of this was the fate of a proposal to hand the police the power to impose alcohol bans for whole towns or cities on football match days. These were dropped not after any moans from fans but because of complaints from the drinks and retail industries – many of whom, I would cynically suggest, pour small fortunes into party political coffers.

Other proposals were included in this bill, which became law in autumn 1999. The term 'football-related offence' was redefined so that anyone convicted of an offence that took place 24 hours either side of the kick-off can be classified as a hooligan. Furthermore, any fans convicted of a football-related offence at home will automatically be given a new international banning order to stop them from travelling to watch England or their club side abroad for up to 10 years. They will have to surrender their passports to a named police station five days before each game. More controversially, the bill also gave the courts the power to punish anyone convicted of an offence abroad. In effect, they would be charged for the same offence twice. Quite right, too, as long as you're guilty, of course – and we all know how reliable both policemen and courts can be both here and overseas, don't we? The problems there are obvious. If you get rounded up or caught in the middle of someone else's trouble, and are arrested, charged and deported, then how are you supposed to prove your innocence back here? What chance would you have of providing credible witnesses at your local court? And what judge in this country is going to decide that, effectively, you were wrongly convicted in a foreign land, with the implications that could have?

Yet even this was not the most dangerous proposal in the bill. For now we have legislation to give the police powers to stop known hooligans travelling abroad even if they do not have any convictions. The proviso being that the police would have to put enough evidence before a court to support their suspicions before permission would be granted. Now call me old-fashioned, but in this country, isn't there the concept of innocent until proven guilty, and doesn't this fly in the face of that? How can a 'known' hooligan not be a 'convicted' hooligan? I'm all for anything that stops hooliganism either abroad or in this country, but if the police have enough evidence to justify the removal of a person's passport, why can't they get enough to convict them in the first place? Only the most naive citizen would believe that once in place, this law would not be extended to cover problem areas away from football and do we really want to hand the police powers of this magnitude?

As far as I'm concerned, the police do not need more powers; what they have to do is use the ones they already have. As anyone who attends matches will know, the preferred tactic of most forces in this country is simply to keep the rival groups apart and hope nothing happens. If anyone plays up they can be thrown in a cell for a few hours and then kicked out once they've cooled down. That way, the arrest figures fall and there are pats on the back all round.

Yet paradoxically, as the arrest figures fell, so the annual bills to the clubs went up, more equipment was developed and new laws proposed. Now why could that have been? To me, the answer to that is obvious, because I have always contended that, in common with various other bodies, the Old Bill are not that concerned about the continued existence of hooliganism. My belief used to be based solely on the fact that not only does the game pour millions into the police each and every year, it provides a very useful training exercise for mounted policemen, dog handlers and riot control into the bargain.

I have now begun to consider something else. Having studied this issue at length, and spoken to many people who have ended up in court for no real reason, it seems to me that football provides an arena for the forces of law and order where they are all but unaccountable for their actions, and they have no reason to want to give it up. Some people will immediately dismiss that last statement, but think seriously for a moment about your average match-day experience. If a policeman used foul language to you outside Tesco's, for example, would you complain? Of course you would. But if he does it outside a ground, you ignore it and simply move on. Or if you were driving along and a policeman pulled you over for no apparent reason and without any explanation, and kept you waiting there for two hours before sending you on your way, you'd have the right hump. Yet things like that go on all the time if you travel away with your club and do you ever complain? No. Even if you did, who would you complain to? If you're on an away trip to Barnsley, for example, is the inspector on the ground likely to give any credence to a complaint from a visiting fan about an officer under his command? More likely he'll simply tell you to piss off.

Let's take it a step further. You're walking into the cinema and a policeman walks up to you, takes off his helmet and smacks you full in the face with it in front of numerous witnesses. You would rightly expect to see him not only in court but in jail and chances are that's where he would end up, especially if the CCTV film was seized and used as evidence. Yet do it inside a football ground, and not only does he get away scot free, you actually end up being charged with affray. What's more, despite the fact that you have a pile of statements supporting your version of events, all of which are totally at odds with the officer's version, you still end up in court. CCTV film of the incident, which was being recorded by the officer's colleagues, is strangely lost and so it comes down to his word against yours and your witnesses'. Even if the case is dismissed, he walks away without a blemish on his record.

Or how about this one: you're walking along and right by the side of the road is a wanted poster with your face on it. You walk into the nearest police station, demand it is removed and threaten legal action into the bargain. They quite rightly shit themselves, apologise profusely and bend over backwards to rectify the mistake. But it's France '98 and you're walking along a road in Toulouse when six English undercover policemen jump on you and deport you for being a Category C hooligan. The fact that you have never even been in trouble before, never mind having any football-related convictions, falls on deaf ears and before you know it, you are back in England. When you complain, you are totally ignored but because you persevere, you finally learn that your status was 'awarded' because you were once photographed in the middle of a particularly nasty incident. Despite the fact that you have evidence to support the fact that you were actually trying to get away from this trouble, it proves impossible to remove this slur on your record, largely because your local MP refuses to take up your cause just in case you turn out to be guilty and make him look a fool. Don't for one second think any of the above couldn't happen, because they all have. Either to me, someone I know or someone I have met, and all within the last 18 months.

All too often, a policeman's version of events will be believed because the second party is a football fan and by association, a football hooligan. So although we should complain about things, in most instances it really isn't worth the hassle. Match days are short enough as it is, so why waste half of it doing something that, chances are, will end up in the bin as soon as you walk out the door? Hence we do not hold the police accountable for their actions at football and that is the real problem. The more individual officers are able to get away with, the worse the reputation and image of the rest becomes.

That lack of accountability extends beyond the individual officer and his treatment of a rank-and-file fan. Who decides, for example, that policing Arsenal for a season will cost in excess of £350,000, or that providing cover for a single Cardiff v Swansea match will cost the home club £15,000-plus? The police do; but who holds them to account to ensure the clubs get value for money? And as football funds and allows the development of a great deal of technology employed by the police at games, what happens to it away from football? Do they still use it and if so, does football have a right to expect a subsidy or even, perish the thought, a rebate from the taxpayer? I don't have the answers to those questions, but surely they should at least be asked.

I am no fan of the boys in blue, as I have said, but I am not on a police-bashing crusade. They have a very important job to do at football and it is one I would not do under any circumstances. But I have stood back and watched them become a police force in the literal sense of the word and I am not happy about it. They have been allowed to manipulate themselves into a position where they can impose their will on the general football-supporting public through enforced early kick-offs, pub closures and rescheduling of games, all under the pretext that a minority of those fans could cause problems. No one calls them to account, no one asks them to explain and they are rarely asked to justify. What's worse, when it all goes wrong, no one, seemingly, ever carries the can.

Never was this more evident than during the last World Cup. For months leading up to France '98, the NCIS had been splashed all over the media telling all and sundry that they knew exactly which hooligans were travelling, how they were getting there and even, in some cases, where they were staying. Should anyone step out of line, they were confident that they would be able to identify and convict the culprits. A few high-profile undercover operations plus the odd dawn raid drew some very favourable and supportive media coverage and suddenly the NCIS profile was sky high. Yet as the tournament approached, their tone became less confident until, the morning after the riot in Marseille, Peter Chapman, then head of the NCIS, appeared at a press conference, shown live on breakfast television, saying that there were people involved that he had never seen before and that his organisation could not hope to identify without a great deal of hard work. So what had they been doing then? How had their confidence been so misplaced and who, if anyone, paid the price with their jobs? Not Chapman, that's for sure; he resigned anyway shortly after the tournament.

As far as I can tell, such questions not only go unanswered but unasked, and that is outrageous. How can we ever hope to deal with hooliganism if the people responsible for enforcing the law of the land can be so obviously inefficient and get away with it?

Shortly after the tournament, when the media finally latched onto the fact that hooliganism was on the increase again, it emerged that intelligence gathering did not extend beyond the 92 professional clubs because the NCIS simply did not have the resources available. This meant that all those lads who ply their particular brand of hooliganism in the non-league game were going about their business pretty much unpoliced. Yet those same lads travel with England on a regular basis. Just because you support a part-time club doesn't mean you cause less trouble; often, these people cause more.

If you place any faith in figures released by the police, it is clear that despite all the talk, things are getting worse. Changes are needed, and fast. As fans, we have to be confident that the police at football are doing the job we need them to do and at the moment that is simply not the case. Much too much time, effort and money is being spent obtaining little in terms of tangible results.

While I would never accuse the police of either fraud or corruption, I would accuse them of indulging in a kind of veiled exploitation. They know better than anyone that they cannot hope to solve this problem and, in the main, all they can expect to do is contain it. Yet they continue to take money from the game, ask for fresh and ever more restrictive legislation from the government and use law-abiding football fans as nothing better than training fodder week in and week out, while continuing to tell us that they are 'the best in the world' at dealing with hooliganism.

If they are the best, it is only because they have had the most practice – and they should not be proud of that claim but ashamed of it.

PART FOUR
The Solution?

———————————

Chapter 10   Getting A Result

Chapter 10

Getting A Result

In a recent interview, a prominent member of the Football Supporters' Association put forward the idea that hooliganism receives a level of attention that is out of all proportion to the actual amount we see in our grounds. This claim was backed up by the statistic that out of almost 25 million people who watched domestic league football during the 1997–98 season, there were only 3,307 arrests; and that the number of people detained at both Liverpool and Everton games during an entire season amounted to fewer than are arrested in Liverpool city centre on a typical Saturday night. On the face of it, this is a valid argument.

But anyone who actually bothers to go beyond the numbers and find out anything about this issue knows they give a false impression. Hooliganism receives so much attention because it *is* a major problem. It impacts on every single football fan in one way or another, damages the reputation of this country and has been a thorn in the side of the game for decades. As a result, it is, as I have said, more important than disabled access, racial abuse, ticket allocations and even the lack of an Asian player in the Premiership. It demands attention and gets it because it is a fascinating and bewildering issue.

One of the questions I am frequently asked is, 'How can we stop it?' The truth is, I do not know. No one does. All I can do, as an average bloke who had a relatively minor involvement in the Saturday lad culture, is put forward my own opinions based on what I believe would have stopped *me* before fear and boredom did that anyway.

The honest truth is that I do not believe we will ever see an end to football hooliganism. It saddens me to write that, but football does not seem to have the will to change. One only has to look back at recent history to see that this is the case. For example, in the aftermath of both Heysel and Hillsborough, the authorities found themselves in a position where the general public would have supported them in whatever they did to drive the hooligans from the game. But both times, they bottled it. After Heysel they merely complained about the ban from Europe, and after Hillsborough they handed over the game to the money men without addressing the culture of intimidation that had caused the tragedy in the first place. Even following Euro '96, when the entire country was in the grip of a football frenzy, the game missed the chance to build on its own success. Instead, it went on an orgy of self-congratulation while the hooligan groups sat back and regrouped.

If football did suddenly discover the will to act, however, then I believe a solution of sorts would be achievable. Although there are many groups who, as we have seen, seem to have a vested interest in the continuing existence of hooliganism, there is one, lone group which badly wants an end to it: the decent, law-abiding football fans. They hold the key. The problem is how to get them into a position where they can use it.

While I stand by my assertion that the game has never really done anything to try to solve this issue, it is fair to say that over the years it has done the odd thing to contain it. Segregation, electric fences, taking people's bootlaces; all these and more have been tried but they have all failed miserably. The reason for that is that the hooligans see every such obstacle as just another part of the hooliganism game, to be overcome. The classic example of that was the idea of banning away fans, implemented at L*t*n just after the Millwall riot in 1985. The club might as well have sent out a challenge to every opposition fan daring them, in effect, to try to get in. Unfortunately, many of the people who rose to that challenge were lads involved in hooliganism and so when they did make it through the gates, they happily announced their presence by causing trouble. Eventually, the whole scheme was dropped but largely because crowds, and therefore income, were dropping.

The problem with ideas such as this is that they only really deal with the problem short-term. While I am all for banning people who cause trouble, we will only ever see a marked decline in football violence when the issue of the Saturday lad culture is addressed. If you removed that, or rather modified it, then we might well see positive steps being taken. But before we look at how that could be achieved, we need to examine some of the ideas that are frequently suggested as possible solutions. Not because they are of any particular use, but because whenever a major incident takes place, they will inevitably be dusted off again by the media.

Some of the more outlandish suggestions I have heard

over the years include such delightful notions as putting them all in a field and letting them get on with it, and even making it law that all male football fans have to be accompanied to games by a female. Such things are not really worthy of comment other than to say that they show just how perverse the general public can be if they set their minds to it. However, the next time we have a major incident, I guarantee that at some point during the post-mortem, the next three proposals will surface: corporal punishment, national service and ID cards. And so, before we get into the real world, we need to look at each of these in brief and explain exactly why, if implemented, they would not have any significant impact on the activities of the hooligans.

During a recent phone-in debate I took part in on Radio 5 Live, a caller offered to flog each and every person detained at a specific game to within an inch of their lives. He even suggested that such a punishment be carried out retrospectively, to cover offences as far back as anyone would want. Leaving aside the obvious lack of sanity present in this gentleman, the case for corporal punishment is one which is often put forward and while it would be easy to simply take the piss and move on, it is something we should look at rather than dismiss out of hand. After all, the next time you find a scratch down the side of your car, the first thing you'll think of is that the person who did it needs a bloody good kicking. The only difference between that kind of justice and corporal punishment is the way that it's administered.

Most people who suggest a return to the use of government-sanctioned violence as a deterrent quote the lack of crime in Singapore, or point to the success the Isle of Man enjoyed when they had birching as a deterrent. However, there is one vital difference. In the case of

Singapore, the practice of flogging was never stopped and therefore, it remains an accepted part of the legal process in that country. Going back to it here would be another thing altogether. I can well imagine that watching someone get the skin lashed off them during the half-time interval would be a good incentive to toe the line, but haven't we come a little bit further than that? Do we really want to return to the good old days of the stocks? Why not go the whole hog and bring back keel-hauling as well?

The case for the reintroduction of national service is stronger. Like the use of corporal punishment, it is often cited as the ideal way to cure not just football's but society's ills. Talk to many of the people who went through it and they will tell you that it instilled in them a sense of loyalty, respect and pride; three things which do seem to be sadly lacking in modern-day Britain. Those same people will also point to the fact that when national service ended in 1963, we saw a marked increase not just in football hooliganism but in problems with British youth generally. Again, on the face of it, their argument is a valid one – but the facts do not entirely support their claim. Football hooliganism, as we have already seen, had been around for many years prior to that and any direct link with the end of national service is tenuous to say the least. And the youth rebellion was already in full swing by the time conscription ended.

As someone who spent over 18 years in the Royal Air Force, I think I am as well qualified as anyone to comment on this issue, and while I do believe that service in HM Forces is an excellent thing, it is not the solution to this problem. There are countless reasons for that, but I would mention four in particular.

The first is that life in the military is not suited to everyone. Leaving your family at an early age is very hard especially if you are not the type of animal who can stand up for themselves.

The second reason is that in these days of equal opportunities, national service would have to apply equally to both males and females. The third reason is that the forces themselves do not want it.

The fourth, and most important, reason certainly with regard to the hooliganism debate, is that it would have no impact whatsoever on any lads who joined up. I was a corporal when I was 'at it' and I have since learnt that I was not alone. Just before I left the forces I spent four months in the Falklands and learnt very early on that there were a number of lads down there with me who had been actively involved with some very well-known mobs on a weekly basis. For many people in the forces, football is their final link not just with their home town but with their mates. When they leave their units at the weekends, where do they go? Football, of course. And if they were a part of a group of lads who occasionally became involved in something, it is unlikely that they would walk away just because of the very remote possibility that they might get into trouble with the Military Police. They might stay in the background for a while, but eventually most would forget their day job and simply carry on as before. (There is, of course, another reason why national service is a bad idea. After all, if every person under 18 faced a spell in uniform, what would happen to all the young professional players? How, for example, would Mr Owen or Mr Beckham fare during a two-year spell in an infantry regiment?)

The bottom line, however, is that we will never see a return to national service in Britain. As with corporal punishment, any government which proposed it would be committing political suicide. If it got to the stage where we had a referendum, we would almost certainly see the highest turn-out of people aged between 18 and 22 ever recorded.

The final idea for tackling hooliganism that we should briefly examine here is the issue of identity cards. Personally, I cannot see the problem with the concept that we should all carry a form of identity with us – I had to for years in the forces and it was never a problem (indeed, on occasions, it was bloody handy). But the very suggestion of it sends the civil liberties groups into apoplexy. Strange, that, given most people in this country happily carry credit cards or driving licences around with them, which are just another form of identification. But again, I cannot imagine what difference carrying an ID card could possibly make to people set on causing trouble at football. The only thing it would do is make it easier to identify them, but that assumes you have been able to catch them in the first place.

An alternative would be for the clubs themselves to set up a national ID scheme, which the government almost forced the game to establish in the late 1980s. Ironically, the people who opposed that scheme the most were the clubs themselves. All they could think about was what effect it would have on the casual fan who did not have a card, and also, most importantly, who was going to pay for it. There were also concerns about the technology involved causing more problems than it would solve (can you imagine the repercussions if the computer controlling entry to Highbury broke down five minutes before kick-off?). The whole idea never stood a chance – though that did not stop the Football Supporters' Association from claiming the credit for blocking it.

Voluntary identity card or membership schemes, set up by a number of clubs in recent years, have enjoyed limited success. But in the main, that has been due to the fact that the mobs have refused to carry cards and so have simply moved to another part of the ground not covered by the membership scheme. No one who had even the remotest involvement with the Saturday scene would carry anything that made it easier for them to be identified. Such schemes are merely token gestures designed to appease the majority of law-abiding supporters.

Given that none of the above ideas either would or has worked, what would? What can football do that might make a difference? To find an answer, we have to look at what options are available not only to the football authorities, or even to the majority of fans, but to the hooligans themselves. For they have a role to play here; they just have to be made to play it.

We know there are no quick fixes or easy answers to football hooliganism because if there were, even the FA would have done something by now. The stark reality is that any resolution would take a massive amount of compromise by everybody involved. Yet at the heart of this problem are the people who cause it, the hooligans themselves. Hooliganism does not exist simply because football is inept, it exists because a small number of football fans set out each and every match day to cause trouble under the banner of their respective clubs. They, ultimately and totally, are to blame. But short of a miracle, there is no way they will simply roll over and stop. And so we have to look at ways in which the game can force them into a position where they give up by choice rather than coercion.

The key here is that football, be it at club or FA level, has to be the body that deals with this issue. For years, successive governments, driven on by the police, have tried to legislate against the activities of the hooligans and they have failed miserably. All that has happened is that the police have accrued more and more laws through which to control everybody else while the hooligans have modified their tactics to work around them. So the time has come to change tack. We have to stop trying to contain and set out to solve.

The first, and most important, step must be for football to face up to the fact that the Saturday lad culture exists under the banner of the domestic game, and for the clubs to accept that and understand that they have to deal with it. Once they have taken that step, the next one is remarkably easy. You have to remove the excuse for violence and in the case of the hooligans, that is going to football matches. The Saturday lads may be a pain sometimes but they are still passionate about the game. However, as I have said, no one has an absolute right to enter a ground so the clubs must use that as a lever to control their own supporters. They must identify their own lads and issue them with a stark warning of what will happen should they step out of line again, either home or away and even outside grounds. Then, if they do, the ban imposed on them must be total and lifelong. Two strikes and you're out.

To be effective, the clubs would have to show that they meant business and were absolutely determined to enforce those bans. That would involve sending spotters to away grounds and making sure that if anyone subject to a ban did sneak in, then they could be identified and thrown out. Once people began to see that the clubs were deadly serious, then it would make a fairly rapid impact on the Saturday culture.

One of the problems the game would face if such a policy were set in place would be from the civil liberties lobby, who would be foaming at the mouth at the idea of people being denied access to stadia simply because they were suspected of being involved in trouble away from the grounds. Well, to be blunt, that's tough. What about the civil liberties of everyone else? What about landlords who have their pubs smashed up, people who are intimidated, or even policemen who receive abuse? Do they not have rights as well? Maybe some of these groups should have a little less concern for the criminal element and a little more for the rest of us. And there is a world of difference between a football club refusing someone entry because they believe that he has caused trouble in their name and, by association, damaged their reputation, and someone having their passport confiscated because the police think he might cause problems abroad. One is the denial of an entertainment (like a nightclub refusing you entry), while the other is a removal of a fundamental right.

I firmly believe that such a system could work, but to be effective it would need to be implemented right across the board. No trials, no studies, just bang! That's it, take it or leave it. If the clubs failed to comply, then the government would have to put pressure on the local authorities to withhold safety licences so that games simply could not take place. If that led to a loss of points, as well as income, then the clubs would quickly get the message.

This would only be the first step as there are other things that need to be done; not just to have an impact on the Saturday lad culture but to have a positive effect on the rest of us. Because the greatest weapon football has in its fight against the hooligans is not the threat of bans, it is peer pressure.

The vast majority of football fans want an end to the activities of the violent and intimidatory minority. Like me, they are fed up with all the shit that surrounds their continuing existence but have grudgingly accepted that there is nothing that they, as individuals, can do about it. That must change. The time has surely come for the decent fans to be given the opportunity to play their part and send a message to the hooligans that enough is enough. I know the very idea of talking to supporters goes against the grain for most chairmen, but in this case it is vital. The concept has worked before – it is how the game dealt with the problem of racial abuse inside grounds. The key to the success of the 'Kick Racism . . .' campaign was that it handed a part of the responsibility to the fans themselves. There are still the odd problems, but when you remember how bad it used to be – black players would run on the pitch to a hail of bananas and monkey chants – it shows how far we have come and how much can be achieved if you can harness the will of the majority. That needs to be done with the hooligan issue, too. We have to change the way that we perceive hooliganism and also the way that the hooligans think of themselves and what they do.

At the moment, being known as someone who is involved in hooliganism has no stigma attached to it at all. Quite the reverse; often those involved are regarded as the good guys, living on the edge and fighting for the honour of the club. The scene still has a trendy image of sorts, what with the designer clothes and the expensive tastes. And as I said before, hooliganism is hardly regarded as a 'proper' crime. The Saturday lads know that and embrace the whole notion that because they fight for their colours, what they are involved in has a perverse kind of legitimacy. We have to change that by making football violence shameful and ostracising those who indulge in it. Nothing will solve this problem faster than a bit of humiliation and embarrassment.

The difficulty here is how you involve the rank-and-file fans in the first place. For in the current climate, most football supporters feel a greater sense of alienation than ever before. Very few of us have any kind of coherent representation at our clubs and none of us have a voice at either the FA or within government, despite the fact that the game is totally reliant on us for its very survival.

We cannot rely on either the clubs or the FA to change their position with regard to customer relations of their own accord, and therefore pressure must be put on them to do so. We have two very powerful weapons at our disposal, but one of them we will never use and the other, for the moment at least, we cannot.

The first thing we could do is to hit the clubs where it hurts and boycott games. We could do that, but we never will. Like all addicts, we need our fix and to miss out on that, even on a point of principle, doesn't bear thinking about. The alternative to boycotting the games altogether is to boycott the catering or even to get ourselves organised and follow the lead of the various Ultra groups in Italy, which we discussed earlier. That would send a clear message to the clubs that we were unhappy. If it went on for long enough, they might even be forced into action to resolve it – might being the operative word. For football is a stubborn beast and even if a club's supporters were able to organise themselves, there is no guarantee that the directors would listen. Indeed, judging by some of the examples we have seen in recent years, at the first sign of supporter solidarity the average board simply digs in and does nothing.

So if we are to force action, then it must be done in a way which the clubs are unable to ignore. And in this country, every football fan over the age of 18 has something which those in authority have to take notice of. It's called a vote.

A few years ago, I suggested the formation of a single issue political lobby group called the Football Party. Initially, the suggestion was that people would stand for their local council to give fans a say in issues that directly affected their local club. It was an approach that proved astonishingly successful in 1990 when supporters of Charlton Athletic FC formed The Valley Party in an ultimately successful campaign to get the club back to their spiritual home.

Such was the response, it quickly became apparent that many supporters believed that this local angle was an idea worth developing. But many people wrote to me and said we had to think big and aim higher. The more I thought about that, the more plausible the whole thing sounded. What finally convinced me that the concept of a national Football Party was a sound one was when I realised that the average local election generates a turnout of less that 40 per cent and that while over 12 million people voted for the Tories in the 1992 general election, approximately 25 million watched the England v Germany semi-final in Italia '90. What this proved to me once and for all was that if you went canvassing around every pub, club, house and factory, and told the electorate that you were standing to give them a say within the football world, there'd undoubtedly be good support, and as soon as the established parties saw there were votes in it, their policies and actions would change so as to give football a kick up the arse.

As a result, I sat down and wrote out a manifesto, one aimed not just at local councils but also at general and European elections. It included four main points. First, the formation of an independent, credible and properly funded body to represent the views and opinions of football supporters from every level of the game; second, the appointment of supporters' representatives to the committees of both the Football Association and the Football Trust; third, the appointment of an elected supporters' representative to the board of every professional football club; and finally, the appointment of an ombudsman or regulator to oversee the activities of the Football Association, the Football Trust, the Premier League and its members, the Football League and its members and supporters' groups.

In August 1998, when it was first released to the press and various supporters' groups, the response was amazing. Yet sadly, the people I wanted to react, the football authorities and the government, paid it little heed. Undaunted, I carried on. More support poured in and the manifesto began to appear all over the Internet. I had enquiries about it from all over Europe and as far afield as Australia. It had certainly captured the imagination of supporters. However, the campaign eventually began to take its toll on me, both in terms of time and finances and I was forced to put it onto the back burner. But the idea is still very much alive and the very fact that so many people continue to respond to it proves that it is sound. It sure would rock the boat were it ever to come off.

The mere idea that football fans throughout the country could even consider voting for a fat git like me proves how desperate they are to be involved in the game they love. Every supporter has a role to play in the future of the game, and that doesn't just apply to the hooligan issue but to every single aspect of football. Every major political party recognises that fact – which is, after all, why Tony Blair does so many stupid photo-calls – but still they do nothing about it. That is not good enough. If football will not provide us with a properly funded platform through which we can be heard and demand answers, then the government must make sure they do. And if *they* don't, that's when we should use our vote, because that is the one thing all politicians are truly scared of. All we need to do is to get organised; but how we actually do that is anyone's guess.

Yet it has to happen. For only by wielding the immense power we as football fans have at our disposal will we ever see an end to the problems facing football, from the hooliganism issue and the asset-stripping to the financial incompetence, greed and sheer hypocrisy of those who supposedly run our game on our behalf. For too long now they have got away with shafting us. They have placed us in danger, sold our very game from under our feet and in far too many cases to note here, have walked away with bank accounts bursting at the seams with money that came out of our pockets. It's not right and the time has come to do something about it.

Conclusion

I talk to a lot of people about the hooligan issue. They range from those who do not even like football to others who were major faces back in the mid 70s. Obviously, the questions they put, as well as the tone of the discussions, vary enormously, but there is one thing that everyone asks me at some point. It is a fairly simple question and until recently, I had a relatively simple answer for it. However, while researching this book, I read through some old files and came across a letter which put that same question but in a very different manner. It said: 'If you had such a good time when you were at it, why are you trying to stop us? You've had your time, this is ours.'

When I read that letter, I sat down and for the first time in ages reconsidered my position on this question. Because while I have been vociferous in my condemnation of football violence, I have a warm affection for the Saturday lad culture that accompanies it. That may seem a contradiction, but it is not. As a football fan, I love being with other football fans, especially English lads, because they are among the most passionate and loyal supporters you will find anywhere in the world. And as everyone should be aware by now, not everyone who acts 'laddy' at football is a hooligan. Yet I have taken a stance against violence at football and will continue to do all I can to force the authorities to eradicate it from our game.

Why should I want to do that? There is not one single answer but many. As a football fan, I am sick of travelling away and having to keep my head down to avoid upsetting the local lads. I want to be able to travel to Stoke, Liverpool or Middlesbrough, walk into a pub for a friendly drink with rival fans and be made welcome rather than abused. And I don't want to be segregated anymore. As fans, we should be able to mingle and enjoy each other's humour and company. Isn't that what being a football fan should be about?

Furthermore, as someone who loves the game, I am sick of seeing it suffer from what amounts to police extortion as a direct result of the continuing existence of hooliganism. How can clubs such as Chester and Exeter hope to survive when they are forced to pay out huge sums because of the activities of a minority of supporters? As fans, we cannot complain about our clubs being in financial strife when we sit back and do nothing while our fellow supporters continue to inflict damage upon them, and therefore ourselves. That simply has to change.

In the same vein, I want to travel to Italy or Germany with England and be welcomed like the Irish and the Scots are. I want to be able to look at the local policemen and not think that I'm about to get baton-charged or deported for no other reason than that I'm English. At the moment, none of these things is possible.

But although each of these is important, they are not the only reasons why I want to see violence removed from football. Some of them are far more personal. For example, as a parent, with a son who is football mental, I will, at some point, have the worry of watching him walk out the door heading off to a game without me. I know it is highly unlikely he would ever get involved in anything and I will watch him like a hawk to make sure he doesn't, but that won't stop me worrying and wondering, because I know how easy it is to become involved and conceal that involvement. My own parents, for example, never knew anything about my activities until *Everywhere We Go* was released. For them, ignorance was bliss; I will not have that luxury.

What I have always tried to do, above all, is to get people thinking. At the back of every non-fiction book I have ever been involved with there has been a request for people to write and pass on their opinions of either the books, hooliganism in general or even the game as a whole. The address is for a post office box and any mail sent to that address is treated with the utmost confidentiality. If it is in any way incriminatory, the details are noted and the letter shredded to avoid any problems for the correspondent should it fall into the wrong hands. Over the years, thousands of letters have poured into that box and, with very few exceptions, they have all been supportive and complimentary. There have been some that have called into question the truth about specific incidents – although it is fair to say that the majority of these have been from people who were on the opposing side and therefore their perceptions are slightly different – while the odd few have called into question my parentage. Yet while every letter is welcome, the ones that always strike a chord with me – and sadly, there have been many – have been sent courtesy of Her Majesty's Prison Service.

I always try to reply to every letter sent to the box but in the case of those that arrive from HMP, I make a special effort to respond as quickly as I can. The reason for that is that as an ex-serviceman I know how important mail can be if you are apart from your family. As a result, I have become a pen pal to numerous lads, many of whom will be behind bars for a long time. I would never condemn, criticise or preach to any of them, but it saddens me that so many decent people have ended up behind bars with their lives, hopes and dreams all but shattered. And for what? Football. It is all so bloody futile.

Do those lads who go to games and get their kicks bullying, intimidating and abusing really understand the full implications of their actions? Do they actually realise what and how much they are risking? That, in an instant, maybe through no fault of their own, they could end up in court or even in prison? Have they any comprehension of what life inside is like, or how hard it is when you come out and have that stain on your life for ever? Do they ever consider the prospect of trying to come to terms with the fact that they threw the bottle that cracked someone's skull and left them brain-damaged or even dead? Sadly, when I go to games and watch the Saturday lads, it is all too apparent that they don't. They have no idea. And their ending up in prison is only one of the alternatives. There is another which is far worse.

Like most people who have ever run with a group of lads, I will happily admit that I enjoyed myself. But as I reminisce about those 'good old days', my mind tends to skim over the worry, the fear and even the pain I experienced at the same time. As we sit in pubs, laughing about times when we steamed down roads, smashed up trains or took ends, or write on the Internet about the clothes and the music that accompanied the Casual scene of the

80s, we tend to forget that every punch that's thrown, kick that's delivered or blade that's flashed has someone on the other end of it. For every violent act there is a victim whose recollection of those same events is almost certainly less humorous than ours. What is more, we forget, or rather ignore, the simple truth that many people have been killed as either a direct or indirect result of football hooliganism, be it the 96 at Hillsborough, the teenage fan who was killed at St Andrews, Matthew Fox at Gillingham or any of the many, many others. Indeed, excluding Bradford, there are 143 deaths mentioned in this book. What a sad and tragic waste it has all been. Is football, or anything else for that matter, really worth that?

If you sit down and think about it, the simple and honest answer has to be no. And once you accept that, how can anyone question why anyone would want to stop it happening again?

Up the 'Ornets.

Appendix

THE CLUBS AND THEIR FIRMS

Aldershot	East Bank Boot Boys
Arsenal	Gooners
Aston Villa	Villa Youth
	Steamers
Barnsley	Five-0
	Inner City Tykes
Birmingham City	Zulu Army
Blackburn Rovers	Blackburn Youth
Blackpool	BRS (Bison Riot Squad)
	Seaside Mafia
	BTS (Blackpool Tangerine Service)
	The Mob
Bolton Wanderers	Billy Whizz Fan Club
	Mongoose Cuckoo Boys
	Tonge Moor Slashers
	The Omega
Bradford City	The Ointment

Brighton & HA	Headhunters
	West Streeters
	NLF (North Lancing Firm)
Bristol City	Inner City Robins
	East End
Bristol Rovers	The Gas
	The Tote
	The Pirates
Burnley	SS (Suicide Squad)
Bury	The Interchange Squad
Cambridge United	Cambridge Casuals
	Pringle Boys
Cardiff City	Soul Crew
	PVM (Pure Violence Mob)
	Dirty Thirty
	D Firm
	Valley Commandos
	The Young Boys
	B Troop
	The Motley Crew
Carlisle United	BCF (Border City Firm)
	BSC (Benders Service Crew)
Charlton Athletic	B Mob
Chelsea	Headhunters
	Shed Boot Boys
	North Stand Boys
	Pringle Boys
	APF (Anti Personnel Firm)
Chesterfield	CBS (Chesterfield Bastard Squad)
Colchester United	The Barsiders
Coventry City	The Legion
	The Coventry Casuals
Crewe Alexandra	RTF (Rail Town Firm)

Crystal Palace	Naughty Forty
	Whitehorse Boys
	Nifty Fifty
Darlington	Darlington Casuals
	Bank Top 200
	The Gaffa
	Under Fives
	The Townies
Derby County	DLF (Derby Lunatic Fringe)
	C Seats
	C Stand
	BBLA (Bob Bank Lunatic Army)
Doncaster Rovers	DDR (Doncaster Defence Regiment)
Everton	Scallies
Exeter City	Sly Crew
	City Hit Squad
Fulham	TVT (Thames Valley Travellers)
Gloucester City	CDB (City Disorder Boys)
Grimsby Town	CBP (Cleethorpes Beach Patrol)
Halifax Town	The Casuals
Hartlepool United	PTID (Pooly Till I Die)
	Blue Order
	Hartlepool ITA (In The Area)
Hereford United	ICF (Inter City Firm)
Huddersfield Town	HYC (Huddersfield Young Casuals)
Hull City	City Casuals
	City Psychos
	Silver Cod Squad
	The Minority

Ipswich Town	IPS (Ipswich Protection Squad)
Leeds United	Service Crew
	YRA (Yorkshire Republican Army)
Leicester City	Baby Squad
	The Wise Men
	MMA (Matthew & Marks Alliance)
	TRA (Thurnby Republican Army)
	ICHF (Inter City Harry Firm)
	BIF (Braunstone Inter City Firm)
Leyton Orient	Orient Transit Firm
	Iced Buns
	Doughnuts
Lincoln City	LTE (Lincoln Transit Elite)
Liverpool	Huyton Baddies
	The Scallies
L*t*n T*wn	MIGs (Men In Gear)
	BPYP (Bury Park Youth Posse)
Manchester City	Guv'nors
	Maine Line Service Crew
	The Borg Elite
	Moston Cool Cats
	Motorway Crew
Manchester United	Cockney Reds
	Inter City Jibbers
	Red Army
	Perry Boys
Mansfield Town	The Carrot Crew
	MSE (Mansfield Shaddy Express)

Middlesbrough	Frontline
Millwall	Halfway Liners
	F-Troop
	The Treatment
	Bushwhackers/Whackers
	NTO (Nutty Turn Out)
	CBL (Cold Blow Lane)
Merthyr	Merthyr Valley Line Firm
Newcastle United	Gremlins
	NME (Newcastle Mainline Express)
	Bender Crew
Newport AFC	NYF (Newport Youth Firm)
	The Trendies
Northampton Town	NAT (Northampton Affray Team)
Norwich City	Barclay Boot Boys
	NHS (Norwich Hit Squad)
	NR1
	The Steins
	C Squad
	C Firm
	ETC (Executive Travel Club)
	The Trawlermen
Nottingham Forest	Red Dogs
	Naughty Forty
Notts County	Executive Crew
	The Bullwell Crew
	Roadside Casuals
Oldham Athletic	Fine Young Casuals
Oxford United	Warlords
	Headington Casuals
	The South Midland Hit Squad
	The 850

	The Oxford City Crew
Peterborough United	PTC (Peterborough Terrace Crew)
Plymouth Argyle	TCE (The Central Element)
	Devonport Boys
	We Are The Lyndhurst
Port Vale	VLF (Vale Lunatic Fringe)
Portsmouth	657 Crew
Preston North End	Leyland Boys
Queen Park Rangers	Ladbroke Grove Mob
	Fila Mob
Reading	Berkshire Boot Boys
	RYF (Reading Youth Firm)
Rotherham United	Rotherham Casuals
	Section Five
Scunthorpe United	The Ironclad
Sheffield United	BBC (Blades Business Crew)
	BBA (Bramall Barmy Army)
Sheffield Wednesday	OCS (Owls Crime Squad)
	Inter-City Owls
Shrewsbury Town	EBF (English Border Front)
Southampton	The Uglies
	Inside Crew
	Suburban Casuals
Southend United	CS Crew
Stockport County	The Company
	Hit Squad
	Stockport Hit Squad
Stoke City	Naughty Forty
Sunderland	Seaburn Casuals
	Boss Lads
	Vauxies
	The Redskins

Swansea City	Swansea Jacks
	Jack Army
	Jack Casuals
	Stone Island Casuals
Swindon Town	Gussethunters
	Southsiders
	South Ciders
	Town Enders
	SSC (South Side Crew)
Torquay United	Torquay Youth
Tottenham Hotspur	Yiddos
	N17s
	Tottenham Casuals
	The Paxton Boys
Tow Law	Tow Law Misfits
Tranmere Rovers	TSB (Tranmere Stanley Boys)
Walsall	SPG (Special Patrol Group)
	Barmy Army
Watford	Category C
	TWM (The Watford Men)
	Watford Youth
West Brom	Section Five
West Ham United	ICF (Inter City Firm)
	Under Fives
	Mile End Mob
Wigan Athletic	The Goon Squad
Woking	Woking Casuals
Wolves	Subway Army
	Bridge Boys
Wrexham	Frontline
York City	YNS (York Nomad Society)

The Crew

DOUGIE BRIMSON

Billy Evans seems a typical East End lad made good; only thirty-two, he runs a successful business in Essex. But Paul Jarvis of the National Football Intelligence Unit knows he's a thug and a villain, and blames him for the death of a fellow police officer. He just hasn't been able to prove it yet.

So when Jarvis finds out that Evans is putting together a hooligan 'Super Crew' to follow England to Italy, he knows that he may finally get his opportunity to put him behind bars – if only he can get someone to infiltrate the Crew and find out what Evans is up to.

Yet all is not what it seems. The Crew believe he is just out to cause mayhem. Jarvis thinks he could be smuggling drugs. But Billy Evans has fooled them all. He has another plan. It is so audacious he knows it will succeed. And it will have catastrophic consequences for everyone concerned.

Except him.

'A winning goal for Dougie Brimson' Lynda La Plante

FICTION / THRILLER 0 7472 7597 4
MASS MARKET PAPERBACK AVAILABLE
FROM MAY 0 7472 6304 3

derby days
the games we love to hate

DOUGIE & EDDY BRIMSON

The local derby isn't just about football, it's about pride, and being able to hold your head up when you go to work on Monday morning, and knowing your lads are better than the other lot. Sadly, the opposite can also be true. The scum up the road can ruin your entire season in ninety gut-wrenching minutes. However, what happens on the pitch is only half the story . . .

From Britain's most authoritative writers on football hooliganism comes a fascinating examination of the passions and emotions that are an integral part of the local derby. *Derby Days* takes a frank but often humorous look at why these games are so important to supporters and examines the lengths to which many will go to put one over their local rivals.

Reviews for their previous books:

Everywhere We Go . . . 'probably the best book ever written on football violence' *Daily Mail*

England, My England . . . 'quite simply brilliant!' *Sky Sports Magazine*

Capital Punishment . . . 'horribly readable' *Time Out*

This book would not have been
possible without the help of football supporters
from all over the country.

If you have any views on the contents of this
book or would like to help us with our football-
related research please do not hesitate to
contact us at the address below.
We will add your name to our database
and send you regular questionnaires on
the issues that affect *you*, the
football supporter.

This is an opportunity to have your say.

All correspondence will be treated with the
utmost confidentiality.

Please write to:
Fandom
P.O. Box 766, Hemel Hempstead, Herts,
HP1 2TU

All students please enclose an S.A.E.